Nigel
All Saints

QUALITIES OF ENDURING LOVE

QUALITIES OF ENDURING LOVE

Edited by

Patrick Whitworth

Terra Nova Publications

Published in Great Britain by
Terra Nova Publications International Ltd
PO Box 2400, Bradford on Avon, Wiltshire BA15 2YN

Registered Office (not for trade):
21 St Thomas Street, Bristol BS1 6JS

Scripture quotations taken from the Holy Bible,
New International Version,
© 1973, 1978, 1984 by International Bible Society.
Used by permission of Hodder and Stoughton Ltd.
All rights reserved.

Cover design by LionHudson
using an original painting
by William Mather

ISBN 1-901949-37-0

Printed in Great Britain at
The Cromwell Press, Trowbridge, Wiltshire

CONTENTS

PREFACE

Enduring love is one of the most important qualities needed in our society today. We appear to have lost the art, to a large extent, in parts of the Western world, of sustaining enduring relationships, and yet it is still the longing of most people to enjoy a married relationship that extends over a lifetime. So in a recent poll 71% of women and 69% of men said that they hoped to have a lifelong relationship with one other person.

The occasion for drawing together these contributions from seven authors was my own silver wedding in the autumn of last year. In September 1979 Olivia and I were married by Sandy Millar in a lovely service in a Hampshire village. So we were especially grateful that he was willing to take part in this series. Twenty five years is still a relatively short time. One couple in England who hit the headlines this year recorded a marriage of over eighty years! But this is not a book about married love alone, although occasioned by it. There are many forms of enduring love toward child, parent, sibling, friends and even colleagues. They are all important to the fabric of our own lives as well as to our community. Many forms of enduring love are under threat today as never before. So this is an attempt to draw out the most significant features of enduring love. The book is written from a Christian point of view; for God the Father's love, expressed through both Jesus and the Spirit, is the most enduring of all loves.

The Psalmist got quite carried away with this thought. In Psalm 136 this refrain is exclaimed twenty six times: His love endures for ever! The qualities of this enduring are one of the main themes of the story of God's love in his creation and in relation to us humans. These qualities are his faithfulness; it is a constant, unchanging, faithful love. It is a covenant making love, fulfilling promises for all time. And what the Father promised, the Son enacted and the Spirit fulfilled. It is love that is attentive to our true needs. It is full of compassion and tender affection. It is a love that changes us into his image. It draws us into the community of the Trinity. It is a love that has offered itself in sacrifice to heal the conflict between himself and his offending child. It is love that always seeks friendship and fellowship. It is a love offered through grace and endless generosity. These are the qualities of God's own enduring love. This small book seeks to explore what these qualities might mean for us in those relationships which rightfully should endure.

I would like to thank all the contributors to this book who first preached on these themes at All Saints last autumn for their enduring commitment to the task. One special contribution is the front cover picture painted by William Mather, until recently the Associate Director of SOMA. I chose a herd of elephants for the picture on the cover as in the natural world they are known for their family love, their protection of the vulnerable and wounded members of their family and for the enduring quality of their being. I would like to thank my publisher, Terra Nova, for their help and encouragement. My thanks also to Gay Carder for transcribing the original sermons. And I would like to thank especially Olivia, my family and friends, for all their enduring love these past years.

Patrick Whitworth

September 14th 2005
Feast of the Holy Cross
—which reminds us of God's costly love for us.

THE CONTRIBUTORS

Patrick Whitworth was Curate at Holy Trinity Brompton, following a first curacy at St Michael-le-Belfry, York, where he served under David Watson. After eleven years as Vicar of Christ Church, Gipsy Hill in South East London, he took up his present post of Rector of All Saints Weston with North Stoke and Langridge. He is presently Rural Dean of Bath, a Canon of Bauchi, Northern Nigeria, and is Chairman of SOMA UK Council. Patrick is married to Olivia and they have four children.

Sandy Millar was the Vicar of Holy Trinity Brompton during the period 1986 – 2005. During that time he led the church to become the largest Anglican congregation in England. The Alpha Course was launched nationally and internationally under his leadership, and at least five church plants were undertaken. Sandy is a Prebendary of St Paul's Cathedral. He currently leads a church plant in Tollington, East London. He is married to Annette; they have four children and several grandchildren.

Nigel Rawlinson is an SSM (self supporting minister) at All Saints Weston, North Stoke and Langridge. He is a Consultant in the Accident and Emergency Department at The Bristol Royal Infirmary, and a teacher in clinical medicine and medical ethics at the University of Bristol. He is married to Pat and they have two daughters.

Sarah Couchman is the Lay Reader of All Saints Weston, North Stoke and Langridge. She is married to James and they have four children.

Peter Norman is an SSM at All Saints Weston, North Stoke and Langridge. Formerly head teacher of a county primary school, he is now retired. Peter is married to Ruth and they have two children and one grandchild.

Alice Cameron-Mitchell was the youth minister at All Saints from 2000 – 2005, leading a vibrant youth work. She is currently completing a theology degree at Trinity College, Bristol.

Tom Peryer, formerly an English teacher, is currently Director of Education in the Diocese of London. He is married to Viola and they have three children.

1

INTRODUCTION

Sandy Millar

It is a great pleasure to introduce this book *Qualities of Enduring Love*. The talks on which it is based coincided with Patrick and Olivia's silver wedding anniversary. I cannot believe that it is twenty-five years since I conducted their wedding, but I am told that there is a lot of evidence for it! Although the subject of marriage is an immensely painful thing for some people for whom it has, for whatever reason, not worked out, this book is a way of helping us all to that quality of enduring love. So I would like to centre our thoughts on verses 10 and 11 of Psalm 85, as we thank God for marriage and faithfulness:

> Love and faithfulness meet together;
> righteousness and peace kiss each other.
> Faithfulness springs forth from the earth,
> and righteousness looks down from heaven.

These words create a lovely picture in which we, for our part, sow faithfulness and God gives righteousness from heaven. Righteousness, as I understand it, is God's ability to put things right and, fundamentally to put us right with himself. These words from the Psalms are a beautiful image of God's covenant relationship with us, and marriage is supposed to be an earthly equivalent of it. So if a young child says, "What is the relationship like between God and us?" you ought to be able to say, "Well, you see, your father and mother are the epitome, with some differences, of his relationship with us." At its centre are the qualities of faithfulness and righteousness, the outworking of his love towards us.

Maybe we cannot control infatuation, but we can nurture that kind of love, and the covenant relationship of marriage is the setting for it. Faithful and enduring love proves good for our health and welfare. However, just to encourage you, there was recently a twenty year study at the University of Warwick of 20,000 men. They found that men with wives live on average three years longer... and earn £3000 a year more!

Dietrich Bonhoeffer made the same sort of distinction between infatuation and love and faithfulness when he wrote to his niece from his prison cell in Germany, as a prisoner under the Nazi regime. She was getting married the next day, and he explained to her that marriage was more than the love the couple had for one another. He went on to affirm that it possesses a higher authority, dignity and power because it is an ordinance of God. In their love the couple only saw their two selves in the world, but in marriage they were "a link in the passing chain of generations". In their love they might only be aware of their own happiness, but as a married couple they would have a responsibility towards "the world and mankind". Whilst their love was their own private possession, their marriage would be more than something personal; it was an "office". Commitment to the marriage and to one another would foster love, rather than the other way round.

So Christians (and of course, marriage is honourable for all) have a particular responsibility, as I see it, to mirror that picture: to set before a man and a wife the task of representing on earth the image of the union between Christ and his church which, of course, is a very high calling. It is an image of faithfulness, of love, and self sacrifice. We practise love, I think, probably through meeting each other's needs. We practise faithfulness through continuing to do so when we do not feel like it. And I think in many ways that that is the issue for our lives today.

Why is it that marriage is in such trouble today? Bob Geldof, speaking on television recently, was endorsing the importance of marriage. Whilst he acknowledged that it might be "uncool" to say so, he observed that every study is clear: dual parenting and upbringing produces healthier and better educated children; and children whose parents are divorced are much more likely to do worse at school, much more likely to commit crimes, much more likely to go to prison and much more likely to commit suicide. He went on to mention that divorced men (he being one himself) tend to live shorter lives than married men, and are statistically more likely to get cancer. He went on to speak of the modern tendency to hop from one lover to another, and suggested that domestic life, with its companionship, nurture, safety and calmness, has been devalued; work tends to be put ahead of home and family life.

"It's all very well," some people will say, "I know that's what we ought to do, and I know that's what we really, really wanted to do when we got married." I do not know any married couple that doesn't intend – really intend – to stick together forever. The question and the challenge is: from where is that determination to stick through everything, and to make it work, going to come? The trouble is, it seems to me, and I am sure it seems to all of us, that the two – love and faithfulness – have been separated. We no longer think of love and faithfulness as being like a horse and carriage, the two going together, inseparable. And today, of course, many are choosing to cohabit instead of getting married. Some see no point in getting married. Some people feel that it is more honest not to make a long-term commitment, because they do not want to make a commitment which they feel that they are not going to be able to keep, and they do not want to add hypocrisy to their other sins.

But intimacy, the building of a relationship, requires vulnerability, and vulnerability requires trust, and trust requires commitment. When we know that the other person will not walk out on us – that they will go on loving us; that they will stay with us through the highs and lows that are part of any relationship – then we begin to be prepared to trust them.

There was an article in a Sunday paper recently, entitled, *How bad does it have to be for you to go?* A man who had been living with a woman for a number of years wrote it, and they had just broken up. He was very honest about it. He wrote that the question in the title of his article was at the back of their minds throughout their relationship. Tragically, it was ultimately the question in the title of the piece that undermined it. To have even the suspicion of that question in your mind can sow seeds of division, supposing as it does that there are some circumstances which love, and the relationship, cannot endure, and the only way through is to separate.

By contrast I came across a woman recently who had lived together with her boyfriend for four years. She described how the relationship had not worked well, and they spent some time apart. They got back together, and two years ago they married. And, quite unprompted really, she said this: "Marriage is so wonderful. Now, we can make plans for the future, because we know that we will be together."

Commitment means we are not going to walk out on each other, if circumstances change. Commitment means we are in this till death us do part, for better, for worse, for richer, for poorer, in sickness and in health. The words are lovely. We are in this, so we want to make it work.

A recent survey of marriage tried to isolate some of the issues that cause tensions in marriage. Money is the greatest cause of argument between British couples, it found, followed by personal habits, children, housework, sex, parents, and friends. From that it follows naturally that couples whose household income is £10,000 or less are twice as likely to argue daily than those with household incomes of £20,000 or more. Well, I don't know whether you would agree with that or not. The most common form of argument is a blazing row followed by a total lack of communication. Couples aged 25 – 34, with children aged up to four years old, have the most arguments, probably because she is at her most stressed and he is at his busiest. Here is part of a peace plan which was suggested: First, make a decision to change what one is doing (so the argument about the dirty sock on the floor must end!) Second, discover the reason why you are arguing. (That dirty sock which was left on the floor!) Third, begin to communicate. (No sulking!) Fourth, resolve the issue. (Removing the sock!) What follows is described as "trouble proofing the future" (promising to use the laundry basket); then acting on what you have discovered or learned. (Avoiding putting socks on the floor again!)

Richard Niebuhr pointed out some years ago that great Christian revolutions happen not as a result of something which was not known before being discovered, but when something that was always there is taken radically. I suppose that when we are working out how we can begin to seek to give God glory for marriage and relationship, for love and faithfulness, and to enable these qualities to flow between us, then I put probably at the top of the list the ability to forgive. This ability to forgive is itself God given; it is part of God's love. Righteousness looks down and shines down, and has the ability to put things right, to start again. But somebody has to say, "I'm so sorry. I am really sorry. I didn't understand that you felt like that." Or, "I did understand that you felt like that, but I thought I could get away with it!"

Winston Churchill, after Dunkirk, said that if we open a quarrel between the past and the present we shall find that we have lost the future. And the ability to start again opens a whole vista of the years ahead. Forgive. But how are we to forgive? Turn back to God. Turn back to God, because God is committed to you.

The late Pope John Paul, whose commitment and concern for the formation and education of young people was well known, speaking to the young people of Krakow some years ago when he was the Archbishop there, reminded them that, "In the Gospels, God speaks of himself, telling us and revealing to us who he is, and who he is in his divinity and his very deepest reality. He says that he is love. He tells how he is love. He is love because he is Father, Son and Holy Spirit. He is love; even within himself he is love. Not only does he speak of himself, but through the Gospels he tells us what he wants. What he wants from us, but first and foremost what he wants *for* us. He says he wants to draw each and every one of us into this love, and involve us in it, which is both a great self revelation and great offer."

When each of us gets steeped back into the love of God, and starts to sense the understanding of the love of God, beginning to enjoy his love and faithfulness, flowing through us from God

18

and back to God and to one another, it is both a calling and a huge blessing. We begin to find out what we need, and that is grace. What John Newton in his beautiful hymn "Glorious things" wrote – and John Newton knew a lot about the grace of God of course – the grace which, "...ever flows our thirst to assuage. Grace, which like the Lord our giver, never fails from age to age." And as that begins to flow, we see, I think, something of what Mother Teresa meant when she gave us her "Plan for Life". Single life, married life —life. "People," she said, "are often unreasonable, illogical, self centred." (That could include husbands I dare say, occasionally! I am sure it does not include wives! It does not say so in the Bible, but in my own case I happily would say that the secret of a happy marriage is a good-natured wife. But as the Bible does not say that, I must not pursue that theme!) What Mother Teresa went on to say was that despite people being unreasonable, illogical and self centred, we are to forgive them anyway. Even if you act kindly you may be thought to have ulterior motives —but continue to be kind. People who are successful may find they have some enemies and false friends; they should nonetheless continue to succeed. The honest may be cheated by others; they should continue being honest themselves. What you build might be ruined by someone else; do not let that put you off building. If you discover happiness, the jealousy of others might be aroused —be happy nevertheless. The good things you accomplish one day will soon be forgotten by others, but you should still keep doing good. The best you give might not be enough for the world, but you are to keep giving it.

You see, in the final analysis it is all between you and God. It was never primarily between you and "them", anyway. But it is of course, between you and them, insofar as it is your husband or wife, insofar as it is your family, insofar as it is the picture that, by God's grace, you are seeking to paint, of God's love and faithfulness.

2

FULFILLING PROMISES

Patrick Whitworth

There can be little doubt that the crisis that faces much of Western society today is to do with enduring relationships.Whereas our forbears were able to sustain enduring relationships, seemingly more successfully than we are today, we are continually confronted with fractures in them which appear all too often as irreparable. Broken families and marriages are far too commonplace in our communities; many children grow up with no or little contact with their fathers.

One church I know is seeking to help a young person whose behaviour, together with that of others, has directly caused many hundreds of pounds worth of damage. Although there is normally a cocktail of causes for such behaviour, much of the reason for young people offending in our towns and villages is due to broken relationships in the home; and although that may not be an excuse for such behaviour, it is certainly a factor. In response to this rising problem of anti-social behaviour in the UK, the government has introduced ASBOs (Anti Social Behaviour Orders) to restrain such young people from criminal damage or personal abuse, but more often than not these are worn like medals by alienated children who seem unperturbed by having them. More recently, the government has adopted the theme of "respect", the buzzword of its domestic administration. But that campaign is rendered less impressive because of the way in which certain members of successive governments have displayed behaviour which has not always matched up to the high standards of personal morality and fidelity to spouses which is still expected of political leaders. Whilst politicians often want a sharp division between public and private life, it must be said that in reality no such division exists, especially given the intense scrutiny now exercised by the mass media. I simply observe that at both ends of the social scale – from government minister to juvenile offender – broken relationships play havoc with lives. They bring politicians down and they lead, as an underlying cause, to the very crime which the politician is trying to curb. So learning to sustain enduring love must be one of the very greatest needs in our society. It is not something which can be legislated for, but it is fundamental to a healthy society.

The chapters of this book are based on a series of talks given at All Saints Weston, on the occasion of our own silver wedding, and that of two other couples in our church. So these addresses celebrate that milestone in marriage. However, whilst recognising that twenty five years of an enduring relationship is still only a short space of time – compared with, say, a carer who has faithfully looked after another for thirty years or more, or a married couple who have been together for sixty years – nevertheless all enduring and continuing relationships have at their centre similar qualities, and these qualities are to be celebrated. I remember a man coming up at the end of a service in which our church had been kindly celebrating our silver wedding and he said, "You do know that you are in the early part of your marriage." He and his wife had been married for sixty three years! What is twenty five among so many years! In this chapter we are thinking of faithfulness to promises —spoken or unspoken.

In marriage, two people make overt promises to each other, but many other relationships have unspoken promises at their root. These other relationships, which are not based on any public ceremony of promise-making as in marriage, are mostly other family relationships —for instance: parent to child, or grandparent to grandchild, or brother to sister or sister to brother, or friend to friend. It is true that no spoken promise is generally made in most of these relationships but nevertheless, at best, there is a deep-seated desire to care for other members of our family as well as friends. These relationships, like the marriage relationship itself, give shape to life, either for good or evil. Where there is care and love these relationships become nurturing and creative, but where this does not exist, or the reverse pertains, then these relationships can cause the greatest degree of emotional pain possible.

Enduring relationships depend on the fulfilment of these spoken or unspoken promises. Professor David Ford in his Lent book of 1997, *The Shape of Living*, describes the fragility of such promises. He rightly points out that they are easily broken but are capable of enduring a tremendous range of suffering, challenges and vicissitudes, and may create lifelong bonds. The key idea he conveys is that promises are the translation of desires into faithfulness, and this central theme will resonate throughout this book.

Promising, or the making of covenants, is the chief way in which God has chosen to deal with humankind. His righteousness and faithfulness is supremely expressed in terms of covenant. One such covenant was first made with Abraham, and is recorded in the critical verses of Genesis 15:5f., when God took Abram, as he was then, outside his tent and, making him gaze at the stars, spoke a word of promise to him, '"Look up at the heavens and count the stars —if indeed you can count them." Then he said to him, "So shall your offspring be." Abram believed the LORD, and he credited it to him as righteousness.' This is one of the seminal actions of the whole Bible, establishing both our human response to God's faithfulness and his call to us, namely to believe in his word of promise, with resulting consequences for all our relationships. God makes a promise, we believe; and the result is being in a right and enduring relationship with God. The promise, which was at first spoken to Abram on that starry night, was later made more tangible and vivid in the Word becoming flesh in Jesus, and God making a promise that if we believe in his Son then we may enjoy the gift of eternal life.

For our purposes here, it is simply worth noticing that the way by which God chose to have an enduring relationship with humankind is through a promise or covenant to which he bound himself. Now, if this is the chosen way by which God enters enduring relationship with those who respond to his promise by faith, it is not surprising that it is through fulfilment of our promises to others that endurance is given to our own relationships.

All of our lives are shaped by promises being either kept or broken. They undeniably influence our lives for good or evil. Twenty five years ago I made a promise to my wife and it went as follows, "With my body I honour you, all that I am I give to you, all that I have I share with you within the love of God, Father, Son and Holy Spirit." It was a promise which needed to be delivered on a daily basis thereafter. As one courier service advertises: "What value are promises if they are not delivered?" Millions have made that marriage promise or something like it to their husbands or wives. Others choose not to make any public promises to another but enter into a relationship based on private agreement. But one of the difficulties with cohabitation or "living together" is that there is no public definition of the commitment to the other person made in the form of a promise. So there is little or no opportunity to enter into a publicly supported relationship. The reasons why so many eschew marriage is because they have lost confidence in their ability to keep the promises, or they feel that in making a promise they might somehow, in almost a superstitious manner, be endangering their relationship in setting up a standard they feel they might be unable to fulfil. And of course they have experienced or seen so many broken promises that they do not want to add further to the number. Such is the profound pessimism about the promises of marriage that increasing numbers avoid it altogether. And as in so much else in our post-modern society we prefer the private to the public. The issue, then, is how promises, which have great power to shape our lives, be fulfilled so as to enable enduring relationships. Any who seek to fulfil their promises will find that there are various problems lurking at the gate, and one of them is dealing with contrary desires.

Dealing with desires

Anyone who is going to mature in their relationships, especially their marriage relationship, will have to learn how to discipline desire. We are all creatures of desire, perhaps more so the male. At the outset there is a heady mixture of physical attraction, mental stimulation, together with the exuberance of finding someone who, wonderfully, is besotted with you. But such high level excitement will subside into an everyday mode. Jack Dominian, in his book *Passionate and Compassionate Love*, has rightly observed that the ecstatic state known as the "falling in love" stage does not last long. The emotional condition of the parties changes, and a different mutual relationship emerges. This is such an important point to make because of the high levels of expectation placed on certain aspects of marriage, particularly romantic attachment, because of the emphasis on that in the modern media. Sometimes one or both parties may not be prepared to live on any basis of mutuality other than that ecstasy initially experienced with the other. If this is the case, they become vulnerable to those desires which have been artificially raised in our culture to levels which no normal human being can satisfy!

So it is quite possible that at some point – after that high state of ecstasy linked with the experience of "falling in love" has cooled – either of the partners may find themselves infatuated with another person. This may coincide with stress, vulnerability or a period of unresolved dissatisfaction with your spouse. For whatever reason, the possibility of infatuation with another is not to be discounted simply because there was a time when you had eyes only for your husband or wife. People change, situations change, you yourself change, and any of these changes can trigger a person to consider satisfying their desires outside marriage.

I remember a vivacious young woman who enjoyed a party and an exciting social life growing tired of her husband because he was seemingly more interested in his computer than her. He spent more time seated in front of it of an evening than talking to her, and no longer had any interest in following her around in a hectic social life. They broke up. Or again, I remember another wife finding her husband boring compared with an able and attractive colleague at work who was paying her a great deal of attention. Although this couple had been sweethearts at university, eight years on, with the demands of children at home, she was finding it hard to resist her infatuation with a colleague at the office. They too broke up. Or again I think of a successful doctor who did not find his loyal and demure wife bringing up their two children exciting enough, and was becoming entangled with his secretary at work. They too broke up. It would be foolhardy of anyone to think that they were not susceptible to the charms of another man or woman who was prepared to flatter them by their attention and provide that frisson of excitement which may not be present in a marriage which bears the strain of childrearing, demanding work and a love which has begun to take the other a little for granted. Infatuations can come along and their power can be very strong. Dealing with them requires a great deal of honesty with ourselves. There may need to be both someone with whom such things can be shared and opportunities with your husband or wife to rekindle that flame of passion which first brought you together. In their very helpful work entitled *The Marriage Book*, Nicky and Sila Lee write about the importance of spending time each week together as well as some days away together each year. It is hard to overestimate the value of such disciplines in married life if some short-lived infatuation is not to take an excessive hold.

But as already stated, promising is that activity which gives shape to our desires. At best, promises are the channels down which our desires may flow safely. If the water of desire is running swiftly and dangerously, and might spill out elsewhere, then the trick is to deepen the existing channel to which we are committed rather than abandon the present one for another. To do this requires discipline and a resolute decision not simply to follow our feelings, however powerful they may seem to be. In the marriage service there is a vital phrase which simply says, "forsaking all others"; to ignore this injunction, or to think that in some way we can maintain more than one relationship, is to fly in the face of the deep human desire to find complete loyalty in our marriage partner. Whoever you are, ignoring this necessity of being exclusively committed to your spouse will only endanger fundamentally the marriage on which you are embarking, especially if your partner is made more vulnerable because he or she was a child of a broken home.

In many relationships couples must weather storms of infatuation. The promises made to another must be the framework for desire and also the bulwark on which fleeting but tempestuous infatuations should crash like waves on well entrenched sea defences. Another kind of storm which promises must deal with are the unexpected disappointments which can threaten the fulfilment of other unspoken promises, not least towards children, who have great power to either thrill or depress their parents.

Overcoming disappointments

It was late one night when the phone call came from the police station. A friend's child had ended up in police custody. He was around fifteen years old, had had a bad patch at school, and his habit of drinking and taking dope had brought him to this point. His father went down to the station to pick him up and take him home. It was the worst moment of that youngster's life. His father did not speak to him all the way home in the car; his father's disappointment was palpable. The temptation for his parents might have been to give up on their son. They had given as much as they knew how; he was throwing away the opportunities of an education and bringing shame on himself and them. This was a test of their unspoken promise of being there for their son whatever. It was equally a wake-up call for the young man, which he would never forget. In this case both parties persevered in their commitment to each other. That teenager did turn a corner and made up his mind to get back to his schoolwork, completing his exams and determining to give up alcohol and drug abuse. And his parents, who had said not a word to him on the night of his return from the police cell, stood by him. They showed their deep disappointment, but only in silence; they did not withdraw their support, helping him to realise his potential. And at the time of writing that is precisely what he is doing.

A scenario like that one occurs with great frequency in families in so many places today. There are lots of disappointed parents and very many testing children. Rob Parsons provides excellent, sound advice in *The Sixty-Minute Marriage*, in which he encourages parents not to be disheartened when they are going through difficult patches with their teenagers, pointing out that for the young people it is tough, too, in that stage in between being children and being adults. He counsels keeping battles to a minimum, and sagely observes that by the time young people reach twenty years of age, they usually begin communicating once more!

Commitments or promises must deal with all kinds of disappointments; that is why in the marriage service we find the vow: "to love and to cherish for better for worse, for richer for poorer, in sickness and in health till death us do part." Whatever disappointments we may have to face, this is a call to go on loving. I look with awe on those who have risen to such challenges in ways you can only begin to guess at, as with a husband who has cared for his wife who was suddenly disabled by a violent attack. I think of a parishioner who looked after his wife who was disabled for nearly twenty years, and who never stirred from a chair in their front room all day. I found his uncomplaining care of her for all those years, springing from his committed love, remarkable. Such people provide living illustrations of what fulfilling promises is all about, and how living out their promises has enabled them to meet superhuman challenges with steady determination.

Promising is the means whereby we translate desire into

faithfulness; promises, or vows, give framework to our living, bulwark to our desires and stability to lives. The old adage that "an Englishman's word is his bond" (or promise) was certainly a golden ideal, whether or not it was actually fulfilled. The idea of both simplicity of speech and fulfilment of our words is scattered throughout Scripture. The writer of Ecclesiastes took the fulfilment of promises seriously: "When you make a vow to God, do not delay in fulfilling it. He has no pleasure in fools; fulfil your vows. It is better not to vow than to make a vow and not fulfil it." He concludes, "Therefore stand in awe of God." (See Ecclesiastes 5:4–7). Of course, for the Jews there were many religious vows which they could make and should fulfil, and no doubt the writer had these in mind. But at root what was abhorred was the light way in which people could make and break promises. The most important promises we have to fulfil are those made to our own family members; fulfilling them is a work of a lifetime and possibly our most important lifetime's work. They are a true demonstration of love. In the next chapter we look at what love is and what it is not.

3

LEARNING TO LOVE

Nigel Rawlinson

And this is my prayer: that your love may abound more and
more in knowledge and depth of insight, so that you may be
able to discern what is best and may be pure and blameless
until the day of Christ, filled with the fruit of righteousness
that comes through Jesus Christ —to the glory and praise
of God.

Philippians 1:9–11

Let us begin with a question: What is it that God intends us to
use to bind relationships together? This question is important
for two reasons. Firstly, the answer gives us guidance about how
we should live with (and for) each other. Secondly, it builds up
and makes Christian relationships distinctive, so that a window
is created through which something of God's work in us may be
seen, and others may be drawn to him. The answer, in a word, is
of course "love"; but by "love" we mean some things which are not
well understood or accepted by many people today. Look again

at the title of this chapter, and note the word "learning" —we are *learning* to love. This sets the agenda, reminding us that we go on learning to love all through life. But it also signals that learning to love has to do with the way of seeking and following God.

First we will think about how we might begin to define love. Then we will look at the three verses above in some depth and apply some of the truths we discover.

How do we even start to define love? There are so many levels. It is a complex word. It includes emotions that we sometimes have difficulty in pinning down. It is hard to say why it is that you are attracted to a close friend. In its primary, biblical meaning, love has to do with self-giving for the good of the other, so the best place to begin looking for a working definition is with examples of different relationships, all of which are important. Think of the relationships of a mother and daughter, of child to child, of father to son, of friends for each other, as well as between husband and wife. Obviously, love concerns much more than that physical expression of love which is sexual love.

In *Captain Corelli's Mandolin* by Louis de Bernières, one scene seems to me to depict most poignantly something of the purity and blamelessness in this love relationship, as well as some other qualities it needs in order to flourish and endure. The story is about a local Greek girl from Kephalonia during World War II. She has fallen in love with an Italian officer, whose regiment had occupied the island. He is lodging with her family. She talks with her father —or at least her father talks *to* her. The father describes love as though it were a medical condition —something like "dementia"! The passionate physical intensity comes and goes, and it is necessary at some point to decide whether you wish always to be together and never apart. More than the immediate desire for sexual relations, real love is deeply rooted and there is a growing together beneath the surface of things. Movingly, the father describes how he and his wife had enjoyed that depth of relationship. Their roots had become so entwined, they found they were one tree and not two.

When we look at "love" in terms of such relationships as these, we see at once that it describes an ongoing process. We go on doing it all our lives. It is about relationships of various kinds with others. Whilst there is a proper love of self (we are to love others *as ourselves*, and when we lack that we find it hard to show love for others), self-giving love is not about focusing on ourselves. It is about the care we have for the other person, and what is for their good.

Our ability to relate with others flows from the way in which we are at peace with ourselves *in the light of Jesus Christ*. When we have that true peace, the peace which the world cannot give, peace in being who we are as adopted children of our heavenly Father, and peace in the awareness of how God is transforming our own lives, then we can relate better to others. Perhaps "love" is starting to sound like something rather arduous! It is not. Whilst we know that the way of love entails sacrifice in greater or lesser degree, loving sacrificially – putting the true good of the other first – is not hard work; rather, it is what flows from the work of the Holy Spirit in us. It is the love of God which we see in Jesus, now operating in us by his grace. This basic understanding of what "love" means should be the bedrock of all our relationships: friendship; affection for our children, siblings, other relatives, perhaps; passionate and romantic love; love for our fellow men and women; love for the outsider, the needy, those God brings to us who he leads us to relate to —all these relationships, without exception, need the foundational element of sacrificial love, which we see, above all, in Jesus, and which, by his grace, operates in us.

Of course, love in this sense often calls for effort on our part. It is not just a matter of feelings. Our feelings do not always lead us to give an immediate, perfect and obedient response to the promptings of the Spirit to do the truly loving thing at once in every situation and relationship, because we are not yet perfect in our obedience and discipleship. We are *learning* to love, and this is part of the process of sanctification —becoming holy. We mentioned the sacrificial character of true love, and that speaks both of the need to work at relationships and of having the *will* to do what is loving and to persevere. If we think of love at work in friendship, we see at once that it is not just a desire (I would like to be friendly with "x"), it is an intention (I am going to be friendly with "x") which is then put into action.

We now turn to the passage from Philippians at the head of this chapter. Paul writes, "And this is my prayer...." He is passionately concerned about his friends in the churches he has formed, so he is praying for them. He may or may not know each one of them intimately; he may not know them at all in a "friendship" sense, but he is praying for them. "And this is my prayer, that your love may abound more and more in knowledge and depth of insight." When people are brought together, when they are united through Jesus Christ, they are living in fellowship together. There is a concept here of increasing in love, abounding more and more, so we learn that love is never static. Whilst the believer's relationship with God is established once and for all, in that we become his adopted children, our awareness of all that this means is growing, because he is teaching us and transforming us all the time. Our relationships with each other change with the passage of time: they should be growing, as we gain greater knowledge of one another and depth of insight. As we get to know each other better, we should be learning to love more as well. And, like Paul, we are to pray for those with whom we relate —from our nearest family members to the people we encounter each day: at work, when out shopping or casually. Any encounter can be used by God, and we may have some completely unexpected opportunity to help someone else to begin to discover the enduring love that God is offering everyone. We are to go on reflecting something of his enduring love in all our relationships.

As we apply this in our lives, it is good to remember three key words that help to characterise love as it is worked out in practice: *respect, vulnerability* and *friendship.* If you set out to *respect* the person you are relating with, and this is reciprocated, there is then a preparedness to be *vulnerable* with each other. Out of this comes a deepening *friendship* for each other. These three words are very relevant in marriage preparation. To replace the word *friendship* with *intimacy* helps define the wonder of good sexual love in the context of marriage. Respect, vulnerability and friendship/intimacy work together.

Paul continues, "...so that you may be able to discern what is best...." What does discernment mean in a relationship? It means that you are looking for what is best in and for the other person. You are seeking to understand that person and something of what they are facing, in the light of God's perfect love for them. What a dramatic difference there is when we contrast this selfless love with a motive of selfish gain. Some people go into a relationship to build up a friendship, because they hope that if they have that friendship then they will get something out of it. That foundation will ultimately fail. Instead, we need to begin to discern what it is that is making the other person be himself or herself —and love them for who they are, not for what we can get from them. We need to appreciate who they are, respect them, and begin to understand them.

We often experience this vividly in the resolution of disagreement. When one has moments of disagreement (and I am absolutely confident that we all know what I am talking about) strange things happen. You know what it is like! Suddenly, in the heat of the moment, you feel strongly about something, and you feel you *know* you are right. You become passionate about the issue, and there is potential for "break up". After a while, and a change in circumstance (maybe you go out for a walk), you calm down, then you come back together. As you eventually resolve the issue there are two phrases that you might find yourselves using: "But I thought you said", and/or, "I didn't mean that". Now what is going on there? "I thought you said ... ahh ... I see"; and, "Oh, so you thought ... no, I didn't mean it that way, I meant it this way." Discernment comes, as you sit down and say, "What was it? What happened there? Let's try to understand each other."

Discernment plays a vital role in the relationship between parent and child, and in this context, I think of the example of a mother and daughter. I have two daughters, and I am learning that daughters can be deep and expressive in their emotions. When *I* notice they have had a bad day, they have had a very bad day! My wife Pat, on the other hand, has a finely tuned ability to discern when there is subtle trouble. Nothing is said, but bags are dumped noisily, people are humphing about the house, and Pat says, "I'm worried." Now I do not have the same discernment. Eventually, usually a bit later on, there is a moment, perhaps just before bedtime, when Pat would go up and say gently, "Right, what's up?" and it all comes tumbling out.

Then our daughter would say, "Mum, how did you know? How did you know that I was upset about that?"

Discernment is a remarkable and wonderful thing in a relationship, helping you to develop a sense about what the other person really needs —and the Holy Spirit can enable us to grow in discernment in ways that may surprise us, as we learn to be open to him, the source of love.

Paul continues, "...so that you... may be pure and blameless until the day of Christ...." "Pure and blameless" —what wonderful words they are in the context of relationships. They almost seem to imply a kind of naïveté or innocence. When we talk about purity and blamelessness in a relationship, in the world in which we live the cynics will object, complaining that life is not like that. But God's will really is that our relationships should have the quality of purity and blamelessness. We do not start out pure and blameless! We come to Christ because we are sinners in need of restoration and forgiveness. By grace, through faith in him, he makes us righteous, and we are now to stay in a place of purity and blamelessness, growing in holiness, repenting whenever necessary.

A relationship which is founded on friendship with God, marked by discernment and mutual care, deals lovingly with conflict, and accords with God's word, is a beautiful and precious thing. Contrast its purity and blamelessness with the world's view of relationships. If, in beginning to define the "love" which we are learning, we have made it all sound rather complicated, then we must affirm that it is not: there is a great simplicity about it, which is reflected in the term "purity and blamelessness". Nevertheless, human experience is complex, and the world delights in making it complex. So you very rarely see dramas on television about a pure and blameless relationship. Most "entertainment" depicts conflict, unfaithfulness and wrongdoing in its many aspects, and the consequences of all that.

Here are two among many possible examples of pressures people face today that come from forces in the world which are ranged against the model of pure and blameless love we have been thinking about. The first concerns a new aspect of bullying in children. Many young children now have mobile phones. OK, they are fashion accessories, but for many children a mobile is a necessity, too, for safety, to contact parents. We have just bought one for that purpose for our twelve year old daughter. We have been warned about a new type of bullying that goes on. What happens is that children of this age learn to text each other. They may text someone they choose not to like that day and say, "You're ugly", and then sign it from that person's best friend. Now, in a moment, the childhood friendship that has built up with purity and blamelessness is sullied by that complexity of deception. Sometimes it is spoiled for ever, because by the time you have gone and investigated and found out who did send the message, and that it was not your best friend after all, there will have been parent conversations, school conversations, you may have been hauled before the head teacher, and that childhood relationship is broken and gone. What a disaster! Isn't that an incredible thing? We really have to look after our children with mobile phones. Their life can be dirtied by the complexities of the adult world in which they live; contrast that with our picture here of growing in love so that you may be pure and blameless.

Consider, too, the relationship between husband and wife, which in the sight of God is a pure and special relationship where two people become one. God's picture of faithful devotion and faithful physical love is described in special passages in the Bible. Contrast that with the world's confused view of sex, which is so disturbing for people who are vulnerable.

We need to celebrate pure and blameless love, especially when it has really endured, so that we can all be encouraged. Recently, we celebrated a golden wedding in my family. Part of that celebration for me is that here were people who had stuck at it and maintained that purity, that blamelessness, and it is special! I see this at the hospital where I work sometimes, in the relatives' room in the Accident and Emergency Department, after somebody elderly dies and I have to go and see their spouse of maybe fifty years or so. That is one occasion when I am vulnerable at work to shedding a tear, because when I am talking to somebody and saying to them that the person with whom they have lived for fifty years has died, the look of "lostness" on their face is huge. And I suddenly realise that I am breaking news about someone and something they have nurtured for their whole lives; something "pure and blameless" has now come to an end.

Another dimension of that purity and blamelessness of which Paul speaks is that when it is lost because of someone's fault it is possible to regain it. Christian forgiveness is a unique thing, as God forgives those who truly repent and we exercise forgiveness of those who have wronged us. Many relationships that become confused and spoilt by the ways of the world, and by our failure, can acquire a new purity and specialness when trust has been rebuilt —the wonder of a faithful relationship restored. With God's grace there is always that possibility of a fresh start.

So Paul prayed that we may be able to discern what is best, we may be pure and blameless until the day of Christ —and, finally, that we may be filled with the fruit of righteousness that comes through Jesus Christ. We are reminded at once of the fruit of the Spirit, which is, "love, joy, peace, patience, kindness, goodness, faithfulness, gentleness and self-control." (See Galatians 5:23.) It is a great list! This is the fruit that we begin to reflect in our relationships as we live in openness to the work of the Holy Spirit in us. And we are all familiar with these verses, "Love is patient, love is kind. It does not envy, it does not boast, it is not proud. It is not rude, it is not self-seeking, it is not easily angered, it keeps no record of wrongs. Love does not delight in evil but rejoices with the truth. It always protects, always trusts, always hopes, always perseveres" (1 Corinthians 13:4ff). They are great words —often used in wedding services, but they can apply to any relationship. As you read them to yourself, it can be a good test – a sort of checklist – sometimes to substitute your own name: Nigel is patient, Nigel is kind, Nigel is not rude, is not self-seeking and is not easily angered.... Pat keeps no record of wrongs! The point is that here we have a passage that helps us reflect on God's intention as we build up friendships based on his love. Those two passages of Scripture truly define and depict real, enduring love.

That love endures not only through time but also despite the unloving attitudes it often encounters in others is illustrated by my last, true story, which concerns a father and son. The son, aged sixteen, was having a real "go" at his father. It was difficult because his mum was in hospital and the son was refusing to go and see her because he was too busy doing other things. And that was the context of the row. I just happened to witness a "real humdinger". They were in firmly entrenched positions, with the son getting alarmingly angry, to the point that he eventually stormed out and drove off on his motorbike. I found the father a bit later on, and said, "What are you going to do?"

He replied, "I don't know, actually. I don't know. But there's one thing I cannot do and that is show him the door."

I remember that very well, because, having heard what his son had said, there was plenty of reason for the father to do just that —if not reflectively, certainly in a fit of pique. Imagine, in the heat of the moment, him saying, "Get out!" But he never did that. He took all that was being thrown at him by his newly independent son, and not once did he say that. This, for me, is a picture of God's love at work, and it worked in that relationship. In time, father and son resolved the dispute, and now, some years later, the family is united and close. In such stories we see enduring parental love, patience and kindness, informed by God's perfect love for us. Such parental love points us toward the infinitely greater, perfect, enduring love of God. Our heavenly Father goes on and on extending his love to each of us.

Learning to love is a process that goes on throughout our lives. I believe we never stop learning. We are to be discerning, to understand and care for the other person. We are seeking purity and blamelessness in relationships. Whatever relationship we are talking about, it is the purity and blamelessness that will be in contrast with the complexities of the world. And as we go on being filled with the Holy Spirit, as the fruit of the Spirit grows within us, we are helped to build God's standard of relationship with each other.

In conclusion, I offer a thought for those who may be on the edge of faith and not sure yet about Christianity: Do not let the lack of love you sometimes see in the institutions of the church distract you from your journey to faith. The media delight in reporting the divisions in churches. Disunity and conflict are "news"! Remember, there is a distinction between believing in God through Jesus Christ on the one hand, and being a member of a church denomination, which is a human institution, on the other.

Much Christian love and understanding is always needed. So do not be distracted by conflict and disunity. The love of Jesus for you personally was perfectly demonstrated on the cross; his church is the great company of all who have come to that cross and received him as Saviour and Lord, and he is our standard. Particular denominations, with all their failings, and individual Christians with theirs, are not the benchmark; we look to Jesus himself.

4

LEARNING TO LISTEN

Patrick Whitworth

There are many aspects of learning to love, and one is listening. I am told that in Chinese the word to listen is made up of two characters, one being the character for an ear, the other for a heart. So presumably to listen is to listen (the ear) into another's heart. At any rate, listening involves both attention and perception— the giving of our full attention to another, together with the perception to interpret what is heard or said or intended. It means not only listening to the spoken word but also observing what is said through the body, whether in the face or signalled by posture, which we call body language. In some situations, that unspoken language may be more indicative of what a person is really feeling than what is actually said, though it must be admitted that there is the ever-present danger of misinterpreting non-verbal clues.

There are few more important skills in any relationship than the will and ability to listen. As someone has aptly observed, we have been given two ears and one mouth, so perhaps we should listen twice as much as we speak! The writer of Proverbs got the measure of it. Here, the "man of understanding" is one who listens with attention and perception:

The purposes of a man's heart are deep waters,
but a man of understanding draws them out.

Proverbs 20:5

In this chapter we are going to look at the vital place that listening has in maintaining our relationships. We cannot overestimate the importance of listening, for by listening we confer dignity on the person we are listening to. One of our daughters went round to visit a family whilst on a holiday in Cornwall. Like us they had three daughters and a son in the family, and the father was also a clergyman. We asked her on her return how she had enjoyed it. "It was great," she said, "and I had a really good chat with David, too."

"Oh, how was that?" I asked.

"Well, he really listened to what I was saying, and asked some good questions, too."

I was pleased, but also challenged. How easy it is for us parents to fail to give proper attention to either our children or spouse—familiarity can breed inattention, and to my shame I know this only too well! In fact, inattention is at root either laziness or indiscipline, because we cannot be bothered to properly listen. Or, worse still, our inattention is selfishness because we are more interested in our own thoughts, schedule and preoccupations, with the result that we do not commit to the discipline of listening. Some people have suffered from an "inattention deficit" all their lives, with devastating consequences. One prisoner attending an Alpha course in a British gaol said, after one of the discussion groups on the course, "It was the first time in my life that anyone has asked what I thought, and then seriously listened to what I had to say."

Some of the writers in the Bible make it absolutely clear that we must listen not only to God, which is a large subject in itself, but also to one another. One of those writers is the brother of Jesus, James, who later became the leader of the Jerusalem church in the years following Pentecost. Much of the teaching in his epistle is about wisdom and how this may be obtained. We are shown that this wisdom may be found through a mature attitude to problems, in which we both learn to pray for wisdom to deal with them (see James 1:5) and develop the ability to listen to one another and to God. Having listened to God in his word, we should put what we are told into action: "Do not merely listen to the word, and so deceive yourselves. Do what it says" (James 1:22). In the midst of this teaching, James helpfully says this on the subject of listening, "My dear brothers, take note of this: Everyone should be quick to listen, slow to speak and slow to become angry..." (v.19). Little did James know that he was giving the dance steps to good and enduring human relationships; from now on it should be "quick, slow, slow". We shall now go dancing!

Quick to listen

Most of us are quick to talk in order to let our views be known, to air our complaint or to tell our story, but instead we are to be quick to listen. Often, we only listen in order to shape our reply rather than truly understand what is being said. Some people are skilled listeners or have cultivated the art of listening through self-discipline. Many people who attain prominence in public life exercise this skill, but of course there may be a self-interested aspect to their use of it. In the context of Christian ministry, good listening skills are vitally important. Unless we can really give attention to others at a very deep level, we are unlikely to be of very much help to them; this involves listening to what the other is saying, and at the same time listening to what the Spirit is saying to us about the person's real need. Our model, as always, is Jesus, whose listening to people shows us what truly compassionate, understanding listening is really like. He gave the most profound answers, not necessarily in the way anyone expected, always full of what the Father was revealing about what underlay the person's question or comment. Although he knew what was in a person's heart, ordinary people could talk to him and ask him their questions —he gave them his time; he gave them opportunity to speak to him; he heard them, and he replied to them without fear or partiality, telling them what the Spirit willed that they should know. That is the model for us: listening in compassionate love, and then sometimes being ready to speak the very words of God into the other person's life, when the time is right.

Scott Peck, in his classic book *The Road Less Traveled*, identifies really listening to and totally concentrating on the other person as manifesting love. He goes on to describe listening in rather an ungainly term as "bracketing" —the idea being that listening requires a double decision: firstly, to set aside our own train of thought, and then, secondly, to take on board the train of thought of another to whom we are listening. To listen is an act of the will. He goes on to point out that to really listen involves putting oneself aside for the moment, as well as accepting fully the person with whom you are in conversation. If the speaker is aware of such an attitude on the part of the listener, it will tend to reduce their own sense of vulnerability, and they become more willing to communicate what is really important to them. Being like this towards another person is demanding and requires love. Peck makes the point emphatically that such truly attentive listening is very much needed, especially between married couples, but often it is absent.

Being quick to listen, therefore, is a willingness to extend ourselves for another by listening to them, which in turn involves being willing to suspend our own preoccupations in favour of their expression or interests.

All close relationships need to be continually sustained by listening, whether we are thinking of husband/wife, parent/ child, lovers, friends or business partners. Because it is quite possible never to really listen to those people who are closest to us and with whom we live, it is probably necessary to make specific times to listen to each other. For the busy pastor it is all too easy to listen to everyone else except those in your own family; for a highly motivated professional or executive it is equally easy to reserve all attention for clients and colleagues and neglect friends and family. Not being listened to is a very common complaint. It is amazing that teenagers frequently say of their parents, "They never listen to me"; and guess what parents say about their teenagers, "They never listen to me"!

So it is essential to make time to listen and talk, not in some artificial way which becomes off putting and stilted, but in a way which is natural, spontaneous and enjoyable. The most natural time for people to talk is over a meal or drink. It might therefore be a good tradition to have a special evening meal once a week when there is time to linger and talk; or to take one of your teenage children out for a pizza on their own; or to go out for an enjoyable activity with your husband; or to do some shared task together in your house or garden —or for someone else. Time set aside to listen and talk is fundamental to the health of any relationship. Availability to the other in marriage is critical to the sustaining of the relationship; it also leads to listening at the deepest level —not only to words, but also to moods.

Jack Dominian, in his book *Passionate and Compassionate Love*, has wisely pointed out that discerning what is going on at a deep level in one's spouse is dependent on our knowing them well. We come to a point when we understand the signals they give: we gain greater understanding of the value they place on things. He goes on to observe that being "read" like that by someone who loves you can remind us of how a parent knew and understood you even before you could talk. We like and enjoy the experience of hearing the person who loves us expressing sympathy or appreciation stemming simply from their awareness of us. That draws two people closer.

This is listening at the deepest level, and can be just as well applied to any relationship with someone we know well, whether relative or friend. The first step in James' "waltz" is, "be quick to listen"; the second movement is, be "slow to speak".

Be slow to speak

Speech has enormous power, James realises. In his epistle he compares the tongue to a bit in a horse's mouth, a small piece of metal which guides a powerful animal. Again, he says it is like a rudder, a small piece of wood which can steer a mighty vessel. Or again, he compares the tongue to a small spark which can set ablaze a whole forest. In each of his vivid illustrations the basic analogy is the same: the tongue representing our speech is a little part of our body but has enormous constructive or destructive power. (See James 3:1–11.) In many ways James is building on the teaching of the Old Testament, especially that found in the Book of Proverbs. Some striking things are said in this book of wise words about both listening and speaking. There are many commands to listen,

"Now then, my sons, listen to me:
pay attention to what I say."

7:24

"Listen, for I have worthy things to say...."

8:6

"Now then, my sons, listen to me;
blessed are those who keep my ways.
Listen to my instruction and be wise;
do not ignore it."

8:32f.

Listening to God is the cornerstone of our discipleship. But we must not only be good listeners (both to him and others) but also good speakers. Words and how we use them are fundamental to any relationship. So, just as there are numerous instructions to listen to the teaching contained in Proverbs, so also there are many encouragements to speak wisely and carefully, and perhaps this is what James had in mind when he taught that we should be "slow to speak". Our speech needs to be considered. So the writer of Proverbs says,

Pleasant words are a honeycomb,
sweet to the soul and healing to the bones

16:24

Or again he gives us that marvellous proverb about speech,

A word aptly spoken
is like apples of gold in the settings of silver.

25:11

In other words, apt words are like a beautiful ornament. Kindness in our speech, gentleness of speech, circumspection and succinctness are all highly prized. (See Proverbs 11:12; 12:22f; 13:3; 15:4; 10:11; 10:19; 15:1.) They adorn and celebrate any relationship.

There are words to avoid in any close relationships which tend only to negativity, such as: "never" or, "always" —and others to use more frequently, such as: "Thank you" or, "You are great." A revealing exercise to try is to check over in your mind the words that you commonly use in conversation with those closest to you. Are the words encouraging or complaining? Are they critical or constructive? It is all too easy to fall into a rut with our speech and not use it to bring encouragement to those around us. When did you last give a compliment to someone at work, saying, "I really admired the way you handled that meeting —there were some very difficult issues to deal with, and you were very adept!" Apparently Mark Twain once said, "I can go a whole month after a good compliment." Imagine what such words can do for a person's self-esteem and confidence. People are far happier when they are confident about themselves in the best way, and we can play a part in helping them to gain confidence. It is another way of extending ourselves on behalf of others which is part of what loving is about. The more confident and encouraged an individual is, the better they function.

It is vitally important to the growth and wellbeing of our children at all stages, including the teenage years, that we try to find positive things to say to them even when there are serious problems to be addressed. If you can find something good and positive to say to encourage them and help them gain appropriate confidence, it will build them up and difficult situations will be more easily de-fused and used as building blocks in a learning process. Most of us respond well to the right kind of praise from those who love us, and that applies most dramatically in our parenting.

Our words have a very significant effect for good or ill on all our relationships. Because we have a propensity to say things which can be damaging, or which we might later regret, and because we hardly ever get round to saying many of the most important things, we know that we need not only to be slow to speak but also to be very conscious of how we are using words in all close relationships —whether at home or in the workplace. And we do well to remember that when the office workers of the World Trade Center were caught in the mayhem, panic and imminent disaster of 9/11, they did not phone home for any other reason than to assure their families, partners or spouses of their love, so that they would have that to hang on to in the bleak years ahead. Be slow to speak but make that speech count. May our words be "sweet to the soul and healing to the bones". The final movement in this dance is the injunction that we should be "slow to become angry" (James 1:19).

Slow to become angry

We can get angry about the slightest thing and sometimes justifiably. One morning, my wife, Olivia, said to me before taking our youngest child to school, "Take the blue car, as yours has no petrol in it."

"Oh, I will be fine," I replied blithely. "I know my gauge; it will do the ten miles to the school with no problem!" I am one of those people for whom the tank is never quite empty, and somehow it will always get you there; but half way up a steep hill, on the other side of our city, the car came to a halt! I rang up and said we were out of petrol, so could she come over and pick our son up and take him to school? How do you think she sounded on the phone? Not exactly delighted, and yes, just a tiny bit cross! Our son was late for school. I was late for a school assembly where I was demonstrating making pancakes, as it was Shrove Tuesday! I was then late for two other appointments and did not get straight again till about 2 p.m.! Yes, we do get angry or mad about all sorts of things —at ourselves, at others; and sometimes, it seems, justifiably so, but the instruction that James gives is to be, "slow to become angry, for man's anger does not bring about the righteous life that God desires."

Whilst there may be many legitimate reasons for feeling angry, we must let go of our anger, otherwise it will become a burden to us. Where an apology has been made, we should forgo anger, release forgiveness and move on. Where there is no apology it is more difficult to let go of anger and forgive, but we should do so for our own sake, as well as for our relationship with the other person. Of course, depending on the gravity of the cause of our anger, it will be either simple or difficult to do. If the offence against us is very serious, it may be hard to relinquish anger and exercise forgiveness, but we must – both for the sake of our own health and, above all, to comply with the firm teaching of Jesus on the matter – otherwise we place an intolerable burden on ourselves.

For a number of years a family had a holiday cottage in a small village. There were only about sixteen residents living in the village, but two of the families would not talk to each other. They were still angry with one other. The cause of their dispute went back many years, to an occasion when one family had forgotten to give the other family a lift to a party. It was a relatively trivial thing which had caused their falling out, but because they had never been reconciled they carried a burden of anger towards each other, so the village of only a few families could never be united. It was a heavy burden for all concerned and, try as others did to unknot their anger, which had now turned into settled resentment, the hoped for reconciliation did not happen. But how many families, neighbours and colleagues have these festering feuds poisoning their relationships.

Some people are slow to anger while others "hit the roof", "fly off the handle", or fall into a rage, at the slightest provocation, so we need to know ourselves sufficiently well to recognise our temperament and our weaknesses in this area. Ideally, we should let go of anger on the same day as it occurs. Paul says: "In your anger do not sin: Do not let the sun go down while you are still angry..." (Ephesians 4:26); and this should especially be the case in family life. Rob Parsons, in his book *The Sixty Minute Father*, tells the story of a daughter coming home one day having dyed her hair orange! Her father was appalled and became very angry, saying that unless she changed her hair back to its natural colour she could not live under the same roof! She refused, and he was left with a no-win situation; either he backed down or she had to move out. As James teaches us, even when severely provoked it is important to be "slow to anger", and recognise teenager boundary pressing for what it is —a period of self-exploration that still needs to know the constant love of parents, however difficult that may be at times. Tattoos, body piercing, hair colour are just milestones along the way! One daughter came to her father and said, "What happens if I muck up? Will you still love me?"

"Of course!" said her father.

"That's OK then," said his teenage daughter. "I just wanted to know" —and then went on with her activity as if it was the most obvious conversation in the world.

The "dance" that James invites us to do is "quick, slow, slow," not a bad series of steps when we consider what we are being asked to do: be quick to listen, slow to speak and slow to become angry. They also provide the right tempo for enduring relationships of love. But alongside learning to listen we must also learn to show affection if relationships are to endure, and to this we must now turn.

5

DEMONSTRATION OF AFFECTION

Sarah Couchman

In this chapter we look at how we actually demonstrate this love, considering not only those with whom we live most closely but also our neighbours, colleagues, friends and family. All around communities seem to be crumbling, but as a church we surely want to be building communities where relationships are genuine and enriching, and will endure.

There are so many important qualities useful for creating relationships that last: really good communication skills, the ability to resolve conflict, maybe a sense of humour – that certainly helps – and letting genuine affection show can be involved in these and much more. But you may think that showing affection is not for you. Some seem to see affectionate behaviour as an optional extra —something for those "touchy-feely" types; simply the icing on the cake. But I am sure that the demonstration of affection is far more integral to a relationship than we realise. A wedding cake without all the beautiful icing is just another piece of fruit cake! The icing helps to make it what it is intended to be. I believe that if we really work at demonstrating our affection to one another, then those relationships that merely exist now, can actually, over time, become quite special. Someone you consider to be an acquaintance might become a special friend. A "good working relationship" can develop into something a lot more enriching, and I am sure it is possible to create a really good marriage where perhaps at the moment it feels like the housekeeper and the butler who happen to be sharing a house together.

We will look at a passage from the Old Testament book, the Song of Songs. This beautiful book was written hundreds of years before Jesus lived on the earth, and it is interesting to learn that when the Jewish people used to come together to celebrate their most important feast, the Passover, this was a book that was traditionally recited, as it was seen as a picture of God's love for his people. Over the years it has been interpreted in many different ways, but what is clear is that it is a series of poems that speak explicitly about the feelings, desires, concerns, hopes and fears of two young lovers. In what follows we will look at the different ways affection can be shown, then see how not to spoil it, and finally think about when to show affection and when to hold back.

Demonstration of affection   *Song of Songs 2:1–2*
This is right at the beginning of the relationship between the Lover and the Beloved, a time of anticipation. The relationship is new and exciting, and the couple are overflowing with love for each other.

> I am a rose of Sharon,
> a lily of the valleys.
>
> Like a lily among thorns
> is my darling among the maidens.

When the girl begins by saying that she is a "rose of Sharon" she is not saying this in a proud or vain way —actually she is being very modest, comparing herself to the very common wild flowers found in that area. We might think of it as being rather like someone saying, "I'm like a daisy or a dandelion." But her lover comes straight back with an affectionate compliment. She may think she is just a common flower, but for him she is special and beautiful, and she is compared favourably with others.

Most of us can remember different relationships, romantic or otherwise, where in the early stages we could barely do enough for each other; everything came very easily. However, most of us recognise that as a stage that passes, or perhaps it is a stage that comes and goes. Even in this short book, Songs of Songs, we later see the couple go through a rocky patch together. It can happen in any relationship: you may know neighbours who have started off having a decent relationship and then a little niggle develops, communication stops and over time a raging dispute ensues; at work, a sense of being devalued can grow into full blown resentment and backbiting; and when we think about what happens in families when we do not feel appreciated, we know the consequences can be even more painful.

So how can we try to avoid such breakdowns?
Let us begin by looking at the word "love". In recent years it has been very popular in Christian writing to make distinctions between different kinds of love (as defined in the Greek), yet Lloyd Carr explains that it is difficult to make that distinction in the Old Testament, because the word for "love" which is used of the marital relationship is also used in loyalty and friendship, as well as in connection with the love God has toward his people. Carr goes on to define love in terms of a disposition within the person which

is shown in actions for the person who is loved.[1] In other words, **love is not just a feeling, but an activity**. That might seem a bit cold to us, because often love is described in terms of a stirring of "fuzzy feelings". Such feelings come and go, but the expression of our commitment and affection for those around us has to stay the same because, even if we are not feeling particularly loving, those people still need to feel that they are special, that they matter, that they are loved. So sometimes we have to *choose* to love, in the same way that we often have to choose to forgive, even though we are not feeling like it.

So how are we actually going to demonstrate our affection for one another? Many people have found the writing of Gary Chapman very helpful. He suggests that there are five different love languages.[2]

The first of these is our use of **words**. Many of us grew up knowing the words "Sticks and stones will break my bones, but words will never hurt me", and most of us have grown up to know that this is a big untruth because words do actually have great power to wound very deeply or, conversely, to really build up. It is lovely to see how giving a compliment to some people can almost seem to cause them to grow by two or three inches! In contrast, it is painful to see a child shrink under the excessively harsh words of a parent. The Bible puts it this way:

> The tongue has the power of life and death....
> *Proverbs 18:21*

So when we are speaking to one another, we need to make sure that we maintain love, gentleness and respect in our tone. We must not fall into the habit of always putting other people down. Sometimes it is fun to be the focus of others' jokes, to be the centre of attention, but if you are always the butt of such "humour", it can be horrible, destructive and actually lead to a loss of a sense of dignity internally. It is important that we build people up, not only in private, but also in public —at home, and with our friends. We need to remember to always affirm, to give compliments (and learn to receive them, too). Remember to say "Thank you", be encouraging, speak kindly to one another and of one another, and ask for things nicely. No matter how long you have known someone or how well, there is no excuse for "grunting" for a cup of tea! Asking nicely and showing appreciation really does make a difference.

Secondly, there is **touch**. Babies need physical affection to grow up healthily. We only have to look at some of those television reports we saw from the orphanages in Romania of withdrawn, unhappy children to see what happens when little ones are neglected in this way. Mother Teresa knew and demonstrated the value of touch as she worked with those who were sick and dying in Calcutta. And we all need, to some extent, to know physical affection through touch. Often people who have been bereaved and lost a husband or wife, say that no one touches them any more, and that is something they really miss —a hand on the shoulder, a little squeeze of the hand would mean so much. And in the course of married life we should not just think in terms of sex and physical intimacy as the only context for showing affection. It should be possible to give a little touch or a protective hug without an expectation of more later on.

Thirdly, there is **quality time**. This means more than just being in the same room together, but total, focused attention on one another.

Be imitators of God, therefore, as dearly loved children and live a life of love, just as Christ loved us and gave himself up for us a fragrant offering and sacrifice to God.

Ephesians 5:1–2

These verses speak of living a "life of love", by pointing us to the supreme sacrifice of Jesus. As we think of his amazing, perfect self-giving love for us, we can be encouraged to grow in self-giving love. Not many of us will literally be asked to give up our lives for one another, but one of the most precious things we do have, and for some of us more precious than money, will be our time, and one of the ways we can demonstrate our love and affection is to give up our time generously to one another. The lie that we always tell ourselves is that a slower day is coming —"I'm just going to get it all done today, and then tomorrow we'll take things more slowly." But that day is never going to come. It is good to make sure that we invest and give time to people right now.

Rob Parsons tells of a letter that a lady wrote to him when she suddenly realised that her family had grown up and left home.[3] In a profoundly moving and poignant way, she wrote of the emptiness of the now empty rooms. Her children had so often asked for her time and attention, but work and other commitments had so often prevented that. Now she longed for the opportunity to hear her children ask her to play with them and do things together. Now she wished she had not been ruled by the phone and had torn up that diary full of engagements. Now she wanted to tell the family how much they meant to her and ask their forgiveness. That account of a desperately sad parent, full of regrets, reminds us to give time to those who are with us now —do not wait until they are about to move on. Nor should you wait until people have died to speak well of them.

Fourthly, there are **actions**, serving one another in practical ways. In a church there are often a handful of visible core members whose work for the church is clearly seen and (usually) appreciated, but often some of the most loving and committed hearts in the church belong to those who come quietly into the building week after week to clean, or to those who faithfully provide refreshments for the rest of us. This is unglamorous and frequently unnoticed service, and yet is incredibly valuable and precious. It is important to serve one another in routine ways, but why not also surprise someone with a one-off act of kindness? A few years ago, during the Golden Jubilee celebrations in our village, there was a big street party in the High Street, largely organised by our local councillor. During the afternoon I had expected to see him walking up and down the street in his suit, congratulating everyone involved. But in the event I saw him in his shorts and tee shirt going around emptying the overflowing bins, and I was touched and impressed by his commitment and care for our community. We need to remember that such acts as taking out the bins at home, or taking a meal to a neighbour during a difficult time, can be extremely powerful means of demonstrating our affection and care.

Finally, there are **thoughtful presents**. Some of us might struggle with the thought of spending money on another as an expression of love. But, of course, presents do not need to be expensive, and we do not have to wait for those special occasions —a little something can mean so much to some people. A friend often brings me a few flowers from her garden, and it gives so much pleasure to have that little vase of flowers on the side in the kitchen for the next few days. A dreary day can be transformed by such a thoughtful gesture.

Consider that list of five again. Think of yourself and ask which of the five you find most meaningful: words of affirmation, touch, quality time, actions or thoughtful presents? We are all different, and each of us responds differently to these different ways of showing affection. It may be that in a relationship one person showers the other with presents, but that person is just longing to hear some kind words. It might be that one works hard in the house, keeping it immaculate, but the other just wants some regular physical affection. We each have a "native" language of love that we find easy to speak and to understand, but sometimes we have to be prepared to speak another's language so that they feel loved and affirmed. That might mean something as simple as stopping to talk rather than getting on with the washing up or some other household task. Only a love that is prepared to speak a different language, to extend itself, will cause a relationship to mature and deepen over the years.

Think of the people you will be meeting tomorrow. How do they feel most appreciated? If you do not know, ask them. Observe what really delights them, and be prepared to act on what you discover.

Reflect on the life of Jesus. He used all five of these languages of love and he is our example. He said, "My command is this: Love each other as I have loved you" (John 15:12).

Do not spoil it   *Song of Songs 2:3–4*
We return to the next few well-loved verses in the Song of Songs:

> Like an apple tree among the trees of the forest
> is my lover among the young men.
> I delight to sit in his shade,
> and his fruit is sweet to my taste.
>
> *v.3*

The girl, the Beloved, picks up on the comparison that her lover has used. Compared to the other young men who are like wild trees of the forest, her lover is like an apple tree. What could she have meant by that? Would her lover have preferred to have been compared to a sturdy oak or a tall cypress? But she is comparing him to an apple tree both because she finds in him a place of safety, security and delight and because he bears fruit. Do people feel safe and secure in our presence, or do they tiptoe around us, afraid that we might blow our rather short fuse, or fear we are going to sink into a deep sulk that can be just as manipulative? Are we the sort of people that others can say hard things to? We can actually undermine all the good we have been doing, all those ways we have been demonstrating our affection, when in a sudden flash of irritation, we lash out, not necessarily physically but in words, and that can leave our well-meant actions looking like rather empty gestures. It does not mean, of course, that we should avoid conflict at all costs, but if we really work hard at this, then it is possible to go through those times of conflict with trust and respect intact. For some of us that will be harder than for others. Some of us are very even-tempered, while others live with real highs and real lows. We need to take responsibility for ourselves, to know ourselves, to know where our weak points are —perhaps when we have allowed ourselves to get really tired, or when we have had that drink too many. We should aim to be that place of security and safety. Verse 4 reminds us of this:

> He has taken me to the banquet hall,
> and his banner over me is love.

Love is displayed for all to see, like a huge military banner flying high. Last summer our town suffered the loss of one of its teachers when he died suddenly whilst on holiday with his family. At his funeral his children had written a tribute that was read out on their behalf. Strikingly, they said that they knew *for sure* that they had come first in their father's life —an amazing tribute to a man who was busy with so many roles, valued by so many different people, and yet his children knew that they came first. We need to make sure that the people around us are so sure of our love and commitment too.

Consider those to whom you are committed or have responsibility. Where do they feel they fall in your priorities? Can you identify your times of weakness, when those close to you may lose their sense of safety and security?

A time to embrace and a time to refrain   *Song of Songs 2:5–7*

> Strengthen me with raisins,
>   refresh me with apples,
>   for I am faint with love.
> His left arm is under my head,
> and his right arm embraces me.
>
> *vv. 5–6*

Clearly this is a place of intimacy and desire, and yet then we come to the next verse,

> Daughters of Jerusalem, I charge you
> by the gazelles and by the does of the field:
>   do not arouse or awaken love
>   until it so desires.
>
> *v. 7*

These verses speak of there being a time to give, and yet sometimes there is also a time to hold back or as the writer of Ecclesiastes puts it, "...a time to embrace and a time to refrain" (Ecclesiastes 3:5). This is a reminder that we should be wise and cautious so that we neither act inappropriately nor fall into sin. Clearly, if we are thinking about children, the vulnerable, or those over whom we exercise authority, there are strict guidelines, and we need to adhere to those. We also need to consider other relationships. When we are starting a new relationship with someone, in our culture a sign of being committed is all too often seen as having sexual intercourse, but as Christians we know that is wrong except between a married couple —God's word prohibits fornication. Then, we often hear people talking about "harmless flirting". Is that accurate? Is it really so harmless? Or is it a dangerously tempting promise of something that cannot be fulfilled, particularly if one party is already married?

A few years ago a friend was having a difficult time in her marriage. She used to say that, when she went to work, in some ways she was looking for someone to be kind to her, and yet she was terrified that if anyone opened their arms to her she might just fall into them. Surely this vulnerability is something many can relate to. We have to be very careful, if we are going to show affection in the form of a bit of "harmless flirting", that we are not actually going to end up hurting someone who is in a very difficult situation in their current relationship.

Quite apart from those times when we would be in danger of abusing our positions of power or influence if we were to demonstrate affection in certain ways, there are also other times when it is right to hold back with our kind acts and gestures. You may recognise the tendency in yourself or another: to try to "buy" affection and love by giving presents or spending time with other people. If we want to show affection for another it should be because we want to give or we are moved by the Spirit to give; we do not give because of what we are going to get back. We need to be very careful not to try to get from someone else what we can only get from God: a really, really deep sense of being loved and valued.

As you consider your interactions with others, ask God to show you if there are any hidden agendas or unfulfilled needs motivating the way that you give out to them.

A word of hope and help

All of this may sound like a very tall order. It is hard to show your affection for other people when you just do not feel like it, if you are feeling tired, if you have been treated badly, or it always seems that it is you having to make the effort. It is hard to channel our pain and frustration in a way that does not leave the other person feeling like a heap on the floor. It is hard to prioritise our time when there is so much clamouring for our attention. And it is hard not to fall into temptation when we feel so low and so starved of love. The good news is that Jesus is just as interested in our relationships as any other aspect of our lives. Integrity, here in our relationships, is just as much a part of living the kingdom of God as when we are out evangelising, interceding and worshipping. Jesus said, "I tell you the truth, no-one can enter the kingdom of God unless he is born of water and the spirit" (John 3:5). When we think about water, we think about cleansing and repentance. The fact is that all of us have fallen in this area, and we know that we have let other people down. We can come in repentance to God and we will know forgiveness. Also, cleansing —some of us have been deeply hurt in this area, and there is a time and space to come to God and be cleansed and healed. When we think of the Spirit, we think of him coming to help and strengthen us, and to help us make the right decisions. But remember that the Holy Spirit enables us to have a relationship with the Father, and the Spirit dwells in believers, assuring us of the reality of that relationship:

> Because you are sons, God sent the Spirit of his Son into our hearts, the Spirit who calls out, *"Abba, Father."* So you are no longer a slave, but a son....
>
> *Galatians 4:6f.*

So as we seek to put into practice the things we have been thinking about, as we demonstrate our affection in ways that are from the heart, appropriate to the particular relationship with the other person, and will be upbuilding for them, the Holy Spirit will help us, strengthen us and empower us; for our part we are to go on being filled with the Spirit.

A few years ago I heard Rowan Williams speaking about love. He said that when we want a child to learn to talk, we do not just leave them alone and then at four or five expect them to be able to talk. We talk to them, and then they will learn to talk. It is the same with love —we should not expect someone to suddenly be able to love. We have to love them and then they learn what it is about. Some of us have had very bad experiences, and our idea of love is warped badly. We need to go back to God to discover what love is all about. When we allow ourselves to be really loved by God, we will receive all that we need right deep down inside.

We have looked at the demonstration of affection, and we see that God's word just overflows with love for his people. If we spent more time reading our Bibles we would discover that. Often, we put off taking time to sit and listen to what he wants to say to us, yet he wants each one of us to know that we are precious, that we are special. We need to spend time alone with him, and as we do so we will find that place of safety and security, of forgiveness and restoration. God's arms are always open to us. Being in relationship with God is a place to be real and to be helped. This is not a place to pretend. And when we allow God to love us in that deep way, then we will be in a position to extend that sort of love to the people around us.

Ask God to open your eyes that you might see the great love he has for you. Seek his forgiveness, cleansing and healing. Let him transform you, and in turn extend that grace to others.

Notes

[1] Lloyd Carr *The Song of Solomon*, IVP, 1984.

[2] In G Chapman *The Five Love Languages*, Northfield, 1992.

[3] Rob Parsons *Loving Against the Odds*, Hodder, 1998.

6

LEARNING TO CHANGE

Patrick Whitworth

What we are thinking about in this chapter is the conduct of change in our relationships. We could do worse than begin with the simple statement that we should concentrate more on changing ourselves into the people God intends us to be, rather than devoting our energies to changing others into what we want them to be. The first half of that sentence assumes there are traits, habits, attitudes which we would do well to consider carefully in ourselves, whereas the second half rightly suggests that we should tread warily when we are considering changing others. We will begin by considering that powerful urge which exists in most of us to try to change other people, and especially our spouses or partners or our children, into the people we think they should be.

Changing others

I am not a psychiatrist but it is something of a truism to say that much of our make-up is due especially to the interplay of our childhood upbringing and our genetic inheritance. Siblings who were split up at the end of the Second World War and sent to Australia with no subsequent knowledge of each other's doings have been amazed, when they were reunited fifty years or so later, to discover that not only do they naturally bear a family resemblance but also may share common interests, and in some cases have even chosen the same names for their children! What accounts for that? This is testimony to the mysterious character of genetic inheritance in families, which only becomes more amazing as we appreciate that those tiny chemical genes can relate to dispositions and tastes, but still we are left free to respond to our own individual environments in an entirely novel way. This may seem a little frivolous, but I was astonished, having assiduously grown beetroot in our vegetable garden for years and found that it was one of my favourite vegetables, to discover that it was also, unbeknown to me, my father's favourite too! What accounts for these strange coincidences —serendipity or something more?

The way in which we respond to our own environment can also be affected by the way in which we have been treated in the early years of life. It is classic psychology to suppose that an individual who is abused or bullied in childhood will himself or herself seek to bully others; or that a boy deprived of his mother in childhood may find it hard to form a mature and deep relationship with one woman, and may search for approval in many relationships in adult life. A chaplain who was working in an institution for young offenders told me that amongst a group of youngsters he was teaching was a late teenager whose earliest memory of his father was using him as an object to break a window of a building, so that the father could commit a burglary! Little wonder, then, that his son ended up in a secure unit, when so deprived of any love or guidance in his upbringing. The abuse a person suffers is so often visited on another. In this context, "healing" can mean breaking into that vicious cycle and enabling new and creative responses. To do that may take years of patient work. In the case of such youngsters, any correction is not accepted for months or even years because they are too insecure to receive it. They may even be unable to agree that a simple sum in maths is wrong because it is seen as another assault upon their bruised and battered egos. Self-esteem is so low that no form of correction can be entertained.

I am not saying that anyone is bound to behave in a certain way – a Christian cannot be a determinist for we, above all people, should know that our God can transform lives – but simply that unsocial behaviour can be much more likely in such circumstances. What all this means is that each of us is influenced both by our inheritance and our childhood, as well as by the ongoing lessons which we learn as we go through life. We are formed by the classic nature/ nurture combination, which in turn in the Christian becomes the arena for the Spirit's work of bringing maturity or wholeness. Our own past experience can also prove to be an engine powering the risky desire we may have to attempt to change the other people who are close to us.

It can be confidently affirmed on good biblical grounds that when it comes to the matter of change within ourselves, the Christian should be at a great advantage. The God who transforms lives has given us what we need, and he goes on giving us more of the power of his Holy Spirit, so the process can continue. The key truths of our Christian faith in this context, which we will look at here, are: that we are accepted; that we are all works in progress; and that we should concentrate more on the change we need to undergo in ourselves, rather than the changes which my parents, my spouse or my children need to undertake so urgently!

We are accepted

The wonderful starting point of the Christian is that we are accepted as we are. (See Romans 5:8.) There really is nothing that we can do to make God love us any more than he already does, and it is also the case that nothing we might do would make him love us any less. His love is perfect and infinite. Of course this is not a reason for doing whatever we like, however contrary it may be to what we know of God's will. As Paul wrote, "What shall we say, then? Shall we go on sinning, so that grace may increase? By no means!" (Romans 6:1f). No, the underlying argument is that if we have truly put our faith in Jesus as our redeeming Lord and surrendered our lives to him, then not only are we accepted but we are changed already. We are not the same. A well-known story about Augustine illustrates this. Before he became a Christian, Augustine had a weakness for women. A little after his conversion, he met one of his erstwhile lady friends. Alluringly, she said, "It is I!" Augustine replied, "It is not I." It may have been mystifying to her, but he knew that he had changed! In another of Paul's letters, he emphatically declares, "Therefore, if anyone is in Christ, he is a new creation; the old has gone, the new has come!" (2 Corinthians 5:17). So not only are you accepted but you become a new creation. It is being this new creation with new desires, hopes and ambitions that keeps us from simply pleasing ourselves and our own instincts at the expense of others.

To understand deep down in your soul that you are not only accepted but also loved by your heavenly Father and Creator is an experience which has tremendously liberating effects upon you, both as an individual and in terms of the way you begin to perceive and relate to others. It meets your very greatest need with God, as you start to live in the relationship with him which he always intended you to have.

It is hard to overemphasise the search for acceptance and love in so many lives. A number of years ago, Mother Teresa, one of the great iconic figures of the end of the twentieth century, spoke perceptively of Western society, when she pointed out how, today, people hunger for understanding love. She affirmed that this was the real answer to loneliness and extreme poverty. That was the reason why the brothers and sisters of her Order could go to countries where the hunger was not for food, such as in the USA, the UK and Australia. For it is in the supposedly wealthy countries that she noticed great loneliness and despair. In these countries many feel unwanted and lack hope or help. Things that contribute to our humanity – such as the ability to smile, and to touch with care – are so often missing from people's lives today. It amounts to a lack of any sense of being loved, understood and respected. She rightly identified those basic human needs.

Twenty years ago David Watson wrote that in our society, which is so overburdened by pressure and expectation, many people need to belong to groups which are caring, accepting and especially marked by Christian love. But the fulfilment of that need is hindered by the feelings people have that they are inadequate. He noted, too, how the the modern media emphasis on sex, good looks and fashion tends to make many people feel even more alone. That is as true today as when he first expressed those views.

The only thing which makes us feel accepted is love —the love of family, friends, fellow Christians and, supremely, the love of God which we meet personally in Jesus. In the Western world, the love of family is all too often broken, thereby allowing our deepest being to be touched by doubt, uncertainty, anxiety, guilt or depression. If we feel unaccepted by those closest to us then we are truly vulnerable to any or all of these emotions. If our friends' support proves fickle, self-seeking or ephemeral, then these feelings are only compounded. It may sound like a cliché to speak of the love of God, but a deep experience of this through accepting the work of Jesus on the cross (where God in Christ showed his love for each of us), and the experience of that love being "shed abroad in our hearts" through the Holy Spirit, really is the prerequisite for knowing in a personal way that God truly loves us, even as we are. God's love, when discovered – or, rather, when it discovers us – accepts us, liberates us, and sets us on the path of change.

We are works in progress

Change can only begin in us when we know that we are accepted and loved; but change, having begun, is in all of us a "work in progress". When I travel in to Bristol on the bus, to go to the city library to write and study, I usually pass a building site on the way into the city. It is interesting to watch the work in progress there. Initially they were clearing the site of debris and rubble from a past building, then they were excavating the site before driving in the foundations with steel uprights and what look like metal cradles, into which concrete will be poured. Presumably these footings will soon support the load bearing columns. You can tell that I am not a structural engineer! Soon the frame will be going up; then the walls and roof. It is very much work in progress, but it is encouraging to see the progress being made from week to week. It also reminds me vividly of what must happen to our lives, and the stages that work must go through: clearing away, digging deep, setting in place the framework, and only later making the building beautiful and useable. Though, of course, the analogy, like all analogies, is far from perfect, for when you become a new creation, God can use you straight away, in new and often surprising ways; nonetheless, his transforming work will continue for the rest of your life. The theological word for this process after conversion is "sanctification".

Sometimes a work of construction can come to a standstill, even when the basic structure is in place, rather like a project in my own city, Bath. Famed for its unique (in the UK) hot water springs, it has long been the hope to have a modern spa, in which residents and tourists alike can bathe in the thermal waters. But at the time of writing the project far from being a "work in progress" appears to be "work at standstill"! Already over two years late in opening and reported to be costing nearly four times its original price, there seems no likelihood of the spa opening in the near future, and it may well cost tens of millions more pounds to complete! It is a depressing case of work making no progress and with no finish in sight! The New Testament makes it abundantly clear that every Christian's life is a "work in progress". And it is desperately sad when that work reaches a standstill because, for whatever reason, we are resisting the ongoing transformation which God wants to bring about in us. The dynamic process of "pressing on" expectantly is illustrated in this passage, in which the apostle Paul wrote of his desire to know both the resurrection power of Christ and the fellowship of sharing in his sufferings:

> I want to know Christ and the power of his resurrection and the fellowship of sharing in his sufferings, becoming like him in his death, and so, somehow, to attain to the resurrection from the dead. Not that I have already obtained all this, or have already been made perfect, but I press on to take hold of that for which Christ Jesus took hold of me.
>
> *Philippians 3:10–12*

Paul had clearly realised that his life was a work in progress.

Likewise, to encourage his readers and teach them how to live and behave throughout this process, Peter wrote:

For this very reason, make every effort to add to your faith goodness; and to goodness, knowledge; and to knowledge, self-control.

2 Peter 1:5

Lastly, John, speaking of the perfect purity of God, and of the hope that the Christian has in Christ, wrote,

Everyone who has this hope in him purifies himself, just as he is pure.

1 John 3:3

Each of these apostles and great teachers of the faith in the New Testament knew, and taught very clearly, there was work to be done in every Christian's life. So we affirm again that rather than constantly pointing out what remains to be done in others' lives, and especially in those closest to us who are hardly going to take kindly to such godly intrusion, we should concentrate on the work to be done in our *own* lives. In a curious way, as we shall see, the more we concentrate on the work in progress in our lives, the better we will sustain our own close relationships. I am reminded of Michelangelo's famous sculpture *The Prisoners* in the Accademia, in Florence. This is, in fact, a series of four sculptures, showing how Michelangelo was able to bring shape and lifelike form from an original block of marble. Gradually, over the cycle of four stones, the sculpture emerges from the stone: first there is the faint outline of the prisoners, and finally the fully formed band of prisoners emerges; thus the figures and the scene become increasingly lifelike. That development begins to depict for me something of the growth and transformation which God can bring about in us. The

Spirit of God is the only true lifegiver. He alone brings genuine life and vitality to people, teaching us more and more the way of Jesus Christ, when we are open to his work in us.

The steps needed to bring change in our relationships are: firstly, to know that we are accepted; secondly to realise that we are works in progress; but, thirdly, to accept others rather than seeking to change them —and then, remarkably, they will change too. This third step is what we must look at now.

Unconditional acceptance

It is important to deal with one misconception right away. By acceptance, I do not mean that everything another does is acceptable or commendable —that every way of carrying on is valid or right. Of course it is not; but what I mean here is that if we give the fundamental impression that we accept and welcome "the other", even if we recognise that they too are "works in progress", then beneficial change is far more likely to occur which will in turn help sustain good relationships. Beneficial change will occur through the knowledge of being accepted, and it may also be that the passing of years as well as the provision of space will enable this good change to take place. In one of his many amusing asides, Mark Twain once said of his father, "When I was a boy of fourteen my father was so ignorant I could hardly stand to have him around. But when I got to twenty-one I was astonished how much the old man had learned!" Who had changed? We are reminded that gaining a new perspective can be a very important part of the process.

Scott Peck, in a rather unusual book entitled *Golf and the Spirit: Lessons for the Journey*, in which he draws an analogy between the game of golf and our pilgrimage with God, speaks frankly of how he had to learn to accept his wife as she was, rather than trying to change her into the person he wanted her to be! He describes the

77

early years of his marriage as being marked by denial of the fact that he and his wife were no longer "in love" in a romantic way; the following five years as including angry discovery of "faults" and efforts to change the other person. For a decade after that, as he describes it, the process was one of futile bargaining, trying to reach agreement on how they would change (which led nowhere); then followed years in which they simply stayed together, without much of a sense that the marriage would survive. Then, miraculously, acceptance of each other came. Each realised that the other's "faults" essentially went with their strengths. As they began to cease attempting to alter their spouse, remarkably they found that they were changing —faster! He describes how things then became better, and has observed how often a couple who stay together beyond a quarter of a century will have learnt some time before to cease their efforts directed toward changing the other person, and will have begun accepting them.

There is, in many of our relationships, an almost instinctive desire to change another person into our own image. If you stand back from this tendency and examine it, how arrogant it is! As if our own way of doing things is infinitely better than the other's way. The issues are not so much issues of morality but more ones of style. But we can object more to someone's style than his or her morals. This tension may exist intensely across the generations, between parent and child. It can exist between families, especially with the in-laws, and it can exist between siblings as well as husband and wife. In most of these relationships it is the perceived different way of going about things which is objectionable, but those very differences are ones that we can learn both to accept and admire. With the passing of time and growing maturity, the differences between us can become reasons for rejoicing, an extension of our own vision of life. But there will need to be a combination of self-discipline, loyalty and patience to get there. Often, many do not find this beneficial change taking place because levels of tension become unsustainable and the relationship breaks up. However, one way of sustaining the relationship and nourishing its existence is by belonging to a nurturing and sustaining community; this, ideally, is essentially three supportive networks of relationships: our family, friends and church. Where each are in place and all are both supportive and sustaining then the hope of working through differences to a point of thriving, rather than merely surviving, is greatly increased.

So the way to bring about creative change relies on three principles. We must understand, deep down, that we are accepted; this may be a lifelong task for those who have been deprived of a nurturing childhood or who have been on the receiving end of different forms of abuse. We need to understand that we are, as Christians, "works in progress" and hopefully not at a standstill —people in whom that image of God is gradually being restored from the point of departure which is true faith in God (and for more on this, read my *Becoming Fully Human*).

Lastly, we must in turn learn to accept others rather than change them, and in so doing we may come to celebrate our differences —truly appreciating our spouse, or the different characteristics of another generation, or the different approach of a brother, sister and in-laws. Putting these three principles into practice is a creative, constructive and continuing approach to the vital challenge of dealing with either our desire for change in others or, more probably, our own need to change. But this is far more easily achieved in the context of community than on our own.

7

BELONGING TO COMMUNITY

Peter Norman

There can be little doubt that the search for community has become one of the great quests of our time. This may be largely the result of the fact that for the last fifty years we have been setting about the steady destruction of community in the pursuit of an individualistic, consumerist society with a privatised morality. The destruction of community results from several forces working to some extent independently of each other, which nevertheless have been near fatal to the sustaining of community in our society. Commercial, technological, moral and indeed global forces have been at work in undermining communities. With respect to consumerism we see, for instance, the local shop replaced by the out of town store; with regard to computer technology we see that some people hardly leave their monitors, creating relationships online but not knowing the person in the apartment next door; with regard to morality, people do what feels right regardless of its effects on others. Of course this is a simplification, but these are all discernible trends and the result is that communities are broken up, whether they be family, neighbourhood or workplace communities. Some may say that we are in the process of replacing one form of community with another, local by virtual, moral by sensual (what feels good) and commercial rather than familial (I am what I wear, not who I was born!) However, such new forms of community, if that is what we can call them, will prove to be ropes of sand. The simple premise of this chapter is that relationships are much more likely to endure if people are part of a community; indeed we were made for communities and outside of them we perish. These communities will be a complex overlapping group of relationships based on family, neighbourhood, church family, friends and colleagues. But we will begin with asking: Why community at all?

The simple answer to that is that we have been made part of God's family. God himself has created this family, and we were created to be part of it. That was his purpose for us even before we were born. As Ephesians 1:5 tells us, "In love he predestined us to be adopted as his sons* through Jesus Christ, in accordance with his pleasure and will...." [*Sons being those who inherit.] Because in his very nature God is love, he treasures relationships, and identifies himself in family terms: Father, Son and Spirit. Relations between the persons of the Trinity, revealed in Scripture, could be said to be God's relationship to himself: he has always existed in loving relationship to himself. So he has never been lonely, and he did not need a family, although his will was to bring one into being. And he planned to create us —to bring us into his family and share so much with us. And this gives God great pleasure. In James 1:18 we read, "He chose to give us birth through the word of truth, that we might be a kind of firstfruits of all he created." When we place our faith in Christ, God becomes our Father; we become his children. Other believers become brothers and sisters, and the church becomes our spiritual family. And is not that, when it sinks in, an amazing privilege?

Hebrews 2:11 says, "Both the one who makes men holy and those who are made holy are of the same family. So Jesus is not ashamed to call them brothers." We are made righteous and holy through Jesus, we belong to him, and that is why our heavenly Father is pleased with us. As we all know, we are surrounded by a world obsessed with status and celebrity, so it is important to remind ourselves of who we are and to whom we belong. Being included in God's family is the highest honour and greatest privilege that we could ever receive. Nothing that the world has to offer even comes close.

So we are called to be God's family, and being part of God's family is a calling to belong. Even in the perfect, sinless environment of the Garden of Eden, God said, "It is not good for the man to be alone...." (Genesis 2:18). And whilst our relationship with Christ is personal, God never intended it to be private. Paul wrote, "...so in Christ we who are many form one body, and each member belongs to all the others" (Romans 12:5). Each member belongs to all the others, so following Christ involves belonging, and not just believing. We are members of his body —the church. C. S. Lewis pointed out that the word "membership", whilst of Christian origin, has since been devalued; certainly its meaning has changed considerably. We recently had a letter from our building society, addressed to "Dear Member", and all they were trying to do was sell us something. But to Paul being a *member* of the church meant being a vital organ of a living body, an indispensable, interconnected part of the body of Christ —and each of us brings our own unique contribution to make up the whole, as we saw in Romans 12:5.

Dietrich Bonhoeffer, in his book *Life Together*, affirmed that the actual presence of other Christians provides great joy, strengthening believers. I wonder, if we are honest, is that our experience? Membership of the church is not a casual option, nor is it something we use only when it suits us. Jesus died for his church, the "body of Christ", the "company of all faithful people" so it clearly matters very much indeed to God, and is part of his plan and purpose. Another picture the Bible uses for the church, stressing its importance, is the "bride" of Christ.

When we belong to the church, we realise that life is meant to be shared; God intends us to experience life together and to go beyond the superficial. In the New Testament, the phrase "one another" or "each other" is used very frequently, referring to unselfish loving, honest sharing, practical serving, sacrificial giving, sympathetic comforting, and many other qualities. For relationships – and particularly love – to endure, we need to be part of a wider community; we cannot do it on our own. It is interesting that in two important services in the church, baptisms and weddings (in their revised forms), the congregation is now asked to make corporate affirmations. In the case of infant baptism, they are asked whether they will support the parents and godparents in their task of bringing up their child or godchild in the way of following Christ. They reply with, hopefully, a resounding, "We will." Similarly, in the wedding service, friends and family are asked whether they will support the couple in the years ahead. They reply with the same response. So both these services now stress the support of the community in both these vital relationships.

After I became a Christian (under the ministry of John Stott, at All Souls, Langham Place), Ruth and I, following our wedding in 1970, went to live in the Club House, the All Souls community centre in the back streets behind Regent Street and Oxford Street. It was the most wonderfully enriching experience as we learned to share our lives with others. We taught together at All Souls school, which is four minutes walk away, and lived and worked among the local community, the school families, and those linked to the Club House. We had a Sunday morning service in the Club House and then we went to All Souls Church in the evening. It was a very supportive community where you very quickly realised that you were not self-sufficient —you depended on one another. And we shared what we had. None of us was very rich in possessions, and we tried to meet each other's needs. We shared meals together, and we shared the pains and the joys of life. It was, for us, a time of real openness and facing reality. If there were problems, you said so. You did not wear a mask and pretend that things were all right. In doing this we learned to accept each other, and learned how to forgive. It was a marvellous and intense time, and it was also great fun. And we certainly made the most of living in the West End. But we also used school holidays to get away, to recharge our spiritual, physical and emotional batteries, and to establish the essential boundaries which prevent burnout.

One of the many valuable lessons we learned from our time at the Club House was that the community requires commitment. Only the Holy Spirit can create real fellowship between believers. But this grows with the choices we make, and how much we are prepared to put into it. Paul underlined this dual responsibility when he wrote, "Make every effort to keep the unity of the spirit through the bond of peace" (Ephesians 4:3). To create a loving Christian community requires both the power of God and some effort on our part. A Christian community is to be marked by honesty, humility and courtesy as we seek to develop our relationships with each other. When issues and problems arise it is much better to face up to them and deal with them, yet so often we would rather not. But if we care enough about the other person or people involved, we will seek to speak the truth in love, not pushing ourselves forward, or setting ourselves up, and being aware of the other person's feelings. For part of our commitment to others is facing reality and seeking to deal with it, as this will deepen our fellowship. If we always gloss over problems and differences, there is a danger that our commitment to each other will be very superficial.

Let us look now at some of the marks of Christian community identified by Paul, particularly in the Epistle to the Romans. From the outset he makes clear that it is all underpinned by love. Love is the hallmark, and love is the driving force in the family of God. In all, between verses 9 and 16 in Chapter 12, he identifies twelve ingredients in his recipe for love. We will look at six of them. The first ingredient is generosity (v.13a). He says, "Share with God's people who are in need." This can mean both to share in people's needs and sufferings and to share our resources with them. This was lived so tellingly by the early church, as we are told in Acts: "All the believers were together and had everything in common" (Acts 2:44). In our self-centred society, true practical generosity of spirit, exercised on a biblical scale, runs counter to the way things are usually done. We have been thinking of our position in the family of God; how generous are we towards our Christian brothers and sisters?

The second of these marks is hospitality (v.13b). Paul says, "Practise hospitality." For if generosity is shown to the needy, hospitality is shown to visitors. This was especially important in Paul's day, since inns were few and far between and those that existed were often unsavoury and unsafe. It was essential, therefore, for Christians to open their homes to travellers and to show the same love to strangers as they did to each other.

The third mark is goodwill (v.14). "Bless those who persecute you; bless and do not curse." Here Paul is anticipating his words in verses 17 to 21, when he deals with our relationship with our enemies, and those who persecute us who are outside the Christian community. And Paul quite deliberately echoes the teachings of Jesus in Luke chapter 6, when he tells us to bless those who curse us and to pray for them. We are therefore called to live at peace with all as far as it depends on us, not giving way to revenge or any kind of evil.

The fourth mark is sympathy (v.15). "Rejoice with those who rejoice; mourn with those who mourn." Loving people is not being aloof from their suffering and joy; to love includes sharing with them at a deep level. We recall the compassion of Jesus —we will be ineffective in our discipleship unless we have some of that compassion in our heart, and learn how to express it.

The fifth one is harmony (v.16a). "Live in harmony with one another." The Greek sentence here means, literally, "Think the same thing towards one another." It reminds us of Paul's appeal to the Philippians, to be like-minded. For since Christians have a renewed mind, it should also be a common mind as to the same basic convictions and concerns. Without that, we cannot live or work together in harmony.

Humility is number six (v.16b). "Do not be proud, but be willing to associate with people of low position. Do not be conceited." Few kinds of pride are worse than snobbery —a concern for status, and looking down on those who are not "one of us". Paul, here, is focusing our eyes on Jesus, who mixed freely and naturally with people from all parts of society, including the outcasts. Clearly, we are to follow his example. So Paul gives us an amazingly comprehensive picture of the love which should mark our Christian communities. He depicts love as sincere, discerning, affectionate and respectful. It is enthusiastic and patient, generous and hospitable, benevolent and sympathetic, and it is marked by harmony and humility. How much happier many church communities would be if that kind of practical quality of love were seen amongst us more and more.

What made our time in the Club House so special was the sense of commitment to a common purpose and to each other. It certainly was not the quality of accommodation, nor any sense of permanence. When we moved in we were given two rooms in a Georgian house to live in, with a shared outside toilet, and were told that in five weeks time builders were to move in and renovate the whole house. Well, four and half years later, they started! We came home from the school one day when the builders had started. "Oh, by the way, we've knocked the outside loo out!" Anyway, eventually we moved out and settled a short time later in Muswell Hill, when I became head of the local primary school.

Within the church there, St James, there was a similar commitment to community, although in a very different setting. Here we were able to experience the same depth of commitment we had in the Club House, in what is one of the smarter London suburbs, and to grow together spiritually as we opened our lives to each other more and more. The main difference between the two was that in Muswell Hill we were far more aware of the other communities in which people were involved on a daily basis – at home, at work, in leisure time pursuits – and we realised that the need was for the principles which governed our Christian lives to be just as relevant outside the church community.

So, how should we seek to apply this to our lives today? We have seen that being part of God's community is a very high calling, and one that he intends (and always has intended) for us. In Old Testament times he called a people to himself, so that he could have a relationship with them. The ideal was that their relationship with him and with each other would enrich other people around, and be an attraction, a beacon of light to those nations round about. And then in New Testament times, the church was created; God called both Jew and Gentile into a community of faith in Jesus Christ. His intention remained to form a people for himself who, in their relationships with him and each other, would shine for him in the world. So as well as setting out the ends, God also graciously provides the means. We belong to other believers; we need them because Jesus drew us into his one body; we are joined to him and to them.

These are wonderful truths that we are called to live out in our daily lives: in our churches, and in all the other communities that we are linked to. How you relate to your church community will influence how you relate to all the other communities in which you live, work and enjoy leisure.

By being real with each other, and living out those ideals which we have seen were set out so clearly by Paul, we have something deeply valuable to offer to others. Being real with each other, being open and honest in love, is I believe the key to establishing enduring relationships. How we do this is of great importance. Sometimes we need to ask others for help. Many of us, and especially men, can be reluctant to ask for the benefit of someone else's experience when we are faced with something perplexing. But surely God has given us and our Christian brothers and sisters the responsibility of providing mutual help for each other. We really are not meant to be just soldiering on alone. Yes, we must go to God in prayer ourselves, and seek his wisdom, his empowering, his plan for our lives; but we also have the community dimension in the body of Christ which means that Christians should use their spiritual gifts to encourage, assist and build up others in the fellowship.

This truth underlines the value of small groups in church life, meeting regularly with people we trust, and to whom we are committed for mutual support and encouragement. Some churches call them discipleship groups, some churches are organized into cell groups, others have different terminology and structures. However we structure this "group" aspect of living in the fellowship of believers, we can draw strength from the fact that Jesus himself established a small group of disciples. His close bond with the twelve influenced and carried over into the relationship with the wider group of followers, as they preached the good news of the kingdom to the needy world around them.

So God made us for community, and he calls us into his own special community, his church, which Jesus Christ died to bring into being, to enjoy him forever —a community created by divine love, which seeks to reflect the love we see in Jesus, and which we know and experience by the operation of the Holy Spirit. What a privilege, and what a responsibility! In a world where community has become increasingly fragmented, and where individualism is the order of the day, we need to ensure that we value our church community; the quality of relationships within it needs to be a priority for each member. It is God's will that we should all be involved. And as we get involved, we find that our own relationships are challenged, nourished and properly and healthily directed. Each person and their special contribution enriches the whole.

8

DEALING WITH CONFLICT

Patrick Whitworth

Almost any relationship will go through moments or periods of conflict: husband and wife, parent and child, brother and sister – or more probably sister with sister or brother with brother – as well as between friends and colleagues. Indeed frustration, anger or resentment may not be far below the surface in an otherwise seemingly charming, self-possessed individual. Some may freely and openly express their displeasure and anger, while others may simply bottle it away until it pours out like Niagara Falls, stunning the recipient who had no knowledge of it lurking, to change the metaphor, like a monster in the deep. The truth is that whilst in childhood we may have easily expressed what we feel, as adults we learn to behave in ways that can hide or disguise our true feelings, sometimes using enormous energy to suppress unresolved anger or bitterness. We become experts in masquerade. On the exterior we may conform to standards of behaviour expected of us, but our closest relationships may give way to behaviour of which, if it were to be made public, we would be thoroughly ashamed! And over time we may fall into those patterns of behaviour in which either it becomes too easy to express anger at the least provocation or it becomes second nature to hide it away.

One of the most important skills we must learn in order to sustain close relationships is how to resolve conflict and deal with anger. Dealing with conflict and resolving the issues and emotions that arise from it is probably the single most important issue facing relationships today.

The most recent UK census (of 2003) shows that 30% of the population are living on their own, and the figure is rising. Although longer-lived pensioners who are living alone account some for some of this, it is also partly due to the increasing number of broken marriages. Divorces in England and Wales are still running at 154,000 a year (in 2004), and 20% of children are in stepfamilies. Few would therefore dispute that dealing with conflict, or to put it positively, continuing trust and openness in relationships, is one of the most critical issues facing the sustaining of enduring love today.

What is true about this on a personal level is true on an ethnic and national level as well. Most of the wars and disputes still causing untold damage and loss of life are the result today of inter-ethnic rivalries or hatreds which both fester and flare, sometimes into appalling violence. We have only to think presently of the Dharfur region of the Sudan, or the Congo, where it is estimated that four million people have lost their lives in recent years, to realise the gravity of ethnic hatred. Differing tribes or people groups, living uneasily with each other in countries whose boundaries were fixed during their imperialist past, resort to violence, often out of fear, with devastating results. Although ethnic disputes are probably the most destructive form of conflict in the world today, in this chapter we must restrict ourselves, by and large, to dealing with conflict in personal relationships. In particular, we will look at the way in the West we have lost the art of sustaining relationships through times of conflict, and how this may be achieved.

Conflict can come in many forms: there are minor irritations and annoyances, which are no more than that; there are rows in marriage over trivial things like putting up the Christmas tree, throwing away things without seeking permission to do so first, staying up late to watch some football match which your spouse has little interest in when she wants to go to bed. These are some things which I have found can be annoying (intensely perhaps) to your partner! However, there are more profound causes for dispute, which need far more resolution. In his helpful book *The Sixty-Minute Marriage*, Rob Parsons tells of an attempted reconciliation between husband and wife after her adultery (which was over). The wife was uncertain as to what to expect her husband's reaction to be. She was extremely surprised that he did not react at all, but just remained silent about what had happened. Eventually, she wrote a letter to him, expressing her desire for him to forgive her. That need is wholly understandable. It is the real, desperate need of anyone who has gone astray in that way, and it is often needed in far more mundane areas of conflict.

In this chapter we will follow a way of resolving conflict based on a pattern taken from Miroslav Volf's book *Exclusion and Embrace*. The pattern follows this sequence of repentance, forgiveness, making space in oneself for the other, healing of memory and finally embrace, with reference to the parable of the prodigal son. We shall begin by looking at the need for repentance, probably in both parties, as the first step to reconciliation or resolution of conflict.

Repentance

As Peter Price (Bishop of Bath and Wells) has observed, repentance is one of the most hopeful words in the English language. However, repentance can seem like an intimidating word to the modern mind. It suggests pictures of sackcloth and ashes, long faces and misery, but in fact it is far more positive than that. In the Bible it is used to mean a willingness to go in an entirely new direction or, to be more precise, to go in God's direction on the assumption that we recognise we ourselves have fallen short in our attitudes and behaviour. As Volf says, "Repentance implies not merely a recognition that one has made a bad mistake, but that one has sinned." It was to this frame of mind that the prodigal came when in the far country, feeding the pods to the pigs. He made up his mind to go to his father and say that he had sinned. The teaching of the Bible does not assume that we can do this on our own. Far from it, the writers of the New Testament are absolutely clear that left to ourselves we cannot achieve this new distinctive direction, which at root means living without ourselves at the centre but with the new desire of following God's will. In fact, repentance means re-alignment; the re-alignment of our lives with the purpose of God for them. This is the basic undertaking which lies at the root of Christian commitment. But if there is an initial and fundamental repentance at the origin of our Christian living, which needs always to be remembered, there are also countless acts of repentance in daily life, where in matters small and large we have to constantly re-align our lives to God's way.

However, the sweep of this call to repentance as the starting point to resolving conflict is probably more radical than we can envisage. Once again, as Volf points out, "The truly revolutionary character of Jesus' proclamation lies precisely in the connection between the hope he gives to the oppressed and the radical change he requires of them." To be blunt, the victim has his own sins and the oppressors have their own sins; both must repent or turn away from them to be truly free and start on the path of reconciliation. It is said that in a phone call some two hours after his release from Robben Island, President Clinton asked Nelson Mandela how he could bear no hatred or resentment towards his oppressors who had incarcerated him for 27 years. He is said to have replied that if he had hatred in his heart the imprisonment would not have truly ended, and anyhow there was work to do now! Understandably, this willingness for both oppressor and victim to repent of their own sins is deeply challenging – perhaps especially to the one who counts himself the victim – and the thought that the victim might have need of repentance is hardly common currency today. Of what sins might either victim or oppressor need to repent? The oppressor should repent of the abuse, aggression or violence they have employed to get their way.

Again Volf says, "The Gospels insist that repentance is not only necessary for the oppressor, but that for them it means more than just purifying desire and mending ways, more even than making restitution to those they have wronged. As the story of Zacchaeus hyperbolically states, repentance entails for them paying back "four times as much" and giving half of their possessions to the poor (Luke 19:8). A genuine repentance of the oppressors will lead to the "injustice" of superabundant restitution, which seeks to offset the injustice of the original violation." If such a notion is then translated into areas of conflict in personal relations or international grievances, what would that mean for the oppressor? What would it mean where trust has broken down because of betrayal in a personal relationship, or where exploitation of a poor producer country has been systematically undertaken to protect the dominance of a rich oppressing one, or where the trust of another has been cynically broken? What will repentance involve here?

Equally, it may be asked, of what type of sins might the victim have to repent? This is a challenging concept. For instance, in the case of physical violence against the person – all too common in cases of domestic violence in the UK – it may mean repenting of any "self-blame", which is a crippling attitude in such circumstances. Such repentance from self-blame will in itself be a journey of understanding. The fact is that any Christian in that position needs to change their mind about their own worth, their own value, in the sight of God, and bring that into line with what the Bible says about them. Self-blame on the part of the victim is not only harmful to the person, it is contrary to the position the person has as a forgiven sinner. Another sin of which the victim may need to repent – if the Spirit shows them that this is in their heart – is hatred: hatred of the oppressor, as well as the resulting desire to inflict corresponding pain. But there is another way, and it begins in every situation of conflict with repentance for the oppressor and the victim alike; without it the imprisonment continues. Those who through God's grace begin with repentance are on the road to freedom. The next step is forgiveness.

Forgiveness

There are only two ways to go when confronted with a personal grievance: either the way of anger, revenge and enmity; or the way of forgiveness, healing and peace. We may know the right way to go, but we need the power to take it.

In his famous book *The Sunflower*, Simon Wiesenthal recalls a pivotal moment in his life. It was about a terrible crisis of forgiveness. He was working in a Polish concentration camp, clearing up rubbish, when a young nurse found him and took him upstairs to the bedside of a young SS trooper whose name was Karl, who had a confession to make before he could die in any semblance of peace. Karl told his miserable story. He had been fighting in a Russian village where a few hundred Jewish people had been rounded up. His group was ordered to cram about two hundred Jews into a house in the village and throw grenades through the windows to set the house on fire. The soldiers were told to shoot anyone who tried to escape. The soldier remembered that behind an upstairs window he caught a glimpse of a man with a child in his arms whose clothing was on fire; the mother stood alongside him. Shielding the child's eyes, the man jumped down to the road, followed by the mother. Karl said that they shot the family, and he told of how that action still haunted him. Turning to Simon, he explained how he felt the need to ask a Jewish person to forgive him, so that he could die in peace. Simon Wiesenthal says he left without saying anything.

Wiesenthal had doubted whether he had the right to forgive the sins of the perpetrator on behalf of the victims. Few of us would ever face such a crisis of forgiveness as the one he faced. The sins committed against our family, or against us, are generally less extreme. But no relationship can exist long without the operation of forgiveness. The path to exercising forgiveness is often marked by hurt first, then anger, possibly sometimes even hate, before the decision to forgive is made. Either we can stay at any of those markers along the way or we can choose to move on to the offering or the receiving of forgiveness. It simply means letting go of the grievance and the emotions that go with it, and being prepared to be at peace with the one who has hurt us. It is a decision, an act of the will. Volf wrote, "Every act of forgiveness enthrones justice; it draws attention to its violation precisely by offering to forego its claims."

Jesus tells us to forgive, and that command applies even if the path to reconciliation is hard. If relationships and love are to endure, then often a child must forgive parent, or a parent child, sibling sibling, husband wife, or vice versa. The power to forgive is probably the single most important need in our relationships today. The fact that so many relationships fracture, leaving people isolated and damaged, is a sign that we have much to learn about this. The path to resolving conflict lies down the way of repentance, the offering of forgiveness, and then making a space for the other person in your heart.

Making space for the other

In the great drama of God's reconciling love at work in Jesus, reconciling a guilty world to himself through the cross (see 2 Corinthians 5:18f), there are two dimensions present: the self-giving love of God, which overcame human enmity while we were still enemies; and, secondly, the creation of space in the divine family of Father, Son and Holy Spirit for each of us. We are welcomed in.

I am sure you have had the experience of someone arriving for a meal at your home who was not expected, or not until the last moment. You hastily go to the kitchen table and lay another place. You literally make a space for them at the family table. God's reconciliation does not leave us out in the cold or in the waiting room —a dutiful handshake followed by a cold shoulder. Far from it, as we shall see, it ends in an embrace. But before the embrace, if it is to be genuine, a place must be found in our heart for the person who was previously estranged. For a married couple it is not good enough to simply agree to live in the same house together, meeting like ships in the night, there needs to be the restoration of intimacy. For parent and child it is not good enough to say that there may be periodic communication without restoration of trust. There must be a making space again in our hearts for the other, and that is a vital step in reconciliation. True forgiveness is not simply drawing a line under a difficult or damaging episode, it is actually going on to make space in our lives for the person who is forgiven.

Recently, I heard of an extraordinary example of this. A criminal who was resisting arrest whilst robbing some premises in order to feed a drugs habit had shot a police officer who had been on duty at the time. The police officer had been badly hurt. The criminal had been arrested, charged and imprisoned. The police officer, a Christian, had visited his attacker in gaol and told him he had forgiven him. Initially, the prisoner had found this hard to accept, but gradually they forged a most unlikely friendship. On his release from gaol they had decided to work together going around schools talking about the risks of possessing knives or firearms, advising on avoiding drugs and crime. In this way their friendship was not only a working partnership of enormous value to the whole community, illustrating the dangers of a lifestyle of abuse, but it was also an extraordinary example of reconciliation and forgiveness. Forgiveness was the gateway to a relationship which had transforming power. It also demonstrates what it means to make space for another who has offended and damaged you.

Healing memories

A few years ago I was talking with a couple of great intelligence and ability, whose daughter was beautiful, capable, lively and very clever. One day, out of the blue, she was murdered. I asked them how they had coped. They said they were given some advice which helped greatly. It did not take away the pain or their suffering, but it enabled them to keep living. They resolved in the aftermath of her death not to talk about their daughter or her tragic loss until the evening of each day, otherwise the emotions of her memory would simply be too overwhelming and nothing else could be thought of or done. It is not possible to forget such trauma, but is it possible for the memories to be healed? It is a big question and there are no glib answers, but surely the Christian faith gives the hope of no longer being imprisoned by hurtful memories.

Damaging events leave memories, and the memories can be a source of unforgiveness. We can trawl through the memories and haul up feelings of bitterness and resentment like so much debris from the bottom of our psyche, but it is essentially a negative pastime. Lewis Smedes, in his helpful book *Forgive and Forget*, writes about this process of dealing with our memories, observing that either they can be dealt with or they can simply provide a fund of continuing negative feelings and attitudes which we can keep revisiting. He says there are two things we can do in this delicate process of memories being healed. Firstly, we can look for new insight about the person who has damaged us, if we know who that is. Gaining some insight into the wrongdoer really can help us to release forgiveness for the evil they did. Hate can then be transformed to pity. Secondly, we can think again about the memory of what has hurt us and armed with this new insight about the person who has damaged us, seek, through God's grace, to wish them well. In biblical terms, we can "bless" the person, as well as forgive them. In all of this, we again remind ourselves that this is not to approve the wrongdoing itself; the offender must make their own peace with God for their offence; but we can release them from any residual blaming, anger and unforgiveness on our part. We must truly decide to forgive what we can forgive, namely the harm we ourselves have suffered.

The daughter of one of the victims of the Brighton bomb, Jo Berry, whose father, Sir Anthony Berry MP, was killed in that

IRA attack, subsequently contacted one of those convicted (who was given multiple life sentences but later released), in order to understand the roots of violence. By trying to understand the motivation of the convicted bomber, but without excusing his crime, she was freed from a purely negative memory of her father's death and so turned a tragedy into something creative.

The hope of healed memories is part of Christian forgiveness. It is a further vital step in the process of reconciliation. The final step in Miroslav Volf's voyage of reconciliation is "embrace".

Embrace

Volf wrote, "Forgiveness is therefore not the culmination of Christ's relation to the offending other; it is a passage leading to embrace. The arms of the crucified are open —a sign of space in God's self and an invitation for the enemy to come in."

As Irenaeus put it, the Son and the Spirit are the two arms of God stretched out to a rebellious world by which humanity was both **made** and then **taken back** into his embrace. (*Against Heresies* 5,6,1). Reflecting this, the Orthodox liturgy celebrating the "feast of feasts" at the end of Paschal matins declares, "This is the day of resurrection. Let us be illumined by the feast. Let us embrace each other. Let us call brothers even those who hate us, and forgive all by the resurrection." So we see that embrace is the end of forgiveness, the object of God's love, and a declaration of Christian intent. It is most poignantly shown in the story of the prodigal son when the father, seeing the son a long way off, "...ran to his son, threw his arms around him and kissed him." (See Luke 15:20). The very act of embrace has four parts: the opening of the arms, creating space for the other and as a gesture of invitation; the opened arms as a moment of waiting, a gesture of vulnerable love still capable of rejection; the folded arms around the other are a gesture of mutual love. ("It takes two pairs of arms for one embrace," Volf wrote); and, fourthly, the reopened arms are a recognition of freedom and individual integrity. Thus, embrace truly offered and received is the end and culmination of forgiveness and the symbol of reconciliation. It is, as it is in the story of the prodigal, the climax of repentance, forgiveness, healing and acceptance. It is the moment of a new beginning, and the supreme test of enduring love.

Note

Quotations from *Exclusion and Embrace*, by Miroslav Volf, 1996, Abingdon Press, Nashville, USA. Used by permission.

9

FRIENDSHIP

Alice Cameron-Mitchell

Journeying together

From ancient times artists and writers have compared the Christian
life to a journey. In recent years some of us in the Christian church
have perhaps over-emphasised the moment of conversion, to the
exclusion of the life-long journey with Christ that succeeds an initial
decision to follow him. As Christians we are called both to journey
towards Christ and to journey with him and this has often been
referred to as "pilgrimage". There is a long history of pilgrimage
in the Christian church, particularly in the Middle Ages, when
pilgrims spent long periods of time away from home travelling
to "sacred places". Pilgrims often faced such hostile conditions
that they rarely travelled alone, offering one another company,
encouragement and protection on their long journeys. Today this
idea of a shared journey is largely an alien concept in our highly
individualistic society, however it should be an essential hallmark
of the life of any Christian disciple.

I spent several years of my life living as part of a Christian community, and three of those years were spent actually living under the same roof with seventy other Christians from about twenty different nations (it was a very big house!) At one stage I shared a room with eleven other girls and I had the top bunk of a triple bunk bed made out of old shipping crates. My bed was literally ten feet from the floor! Just imagine living with other Christians all the time —shared values, shared vision, no conflict... heaven on earth. Well, not quite! I learned pretty quickly that just because I was living with other Christians, it did not guarantee the absence of conflict, nor even shared vision and values, particularly if those values were culture specific! However, living as part of this community was a formative experience for me and I learned lessons I have never forgotten about interdependence and what it might mean to have a shared journey, warts and all, with others. It was a great privilege to see each other grow in character and maturity as we were forced to face all sorts of issues that were thrown up in our own lives, through living in such close proximity to one another.

The eighteenth century evangelist John Wesley once said, "There is no such thing as solitary religion," and yet for so many of us our experience of the Christian life is a very solitary one. So much of what we sing and so much of what we hear being taught is about "me" and "my relationship with God". Of course there is truth in this but it is only part of God's intention for us as his people. In fact hardly any of the teaching in the New Testament is directed to individuals, and most of the instructional verbs given to the followers of Christ were plural verbs. The New Testament teaching of the church as a "body",[1] makes it clear that we are just not made to live the Christian life in isolation from one another, we are created to need each other at the most fundamental level.

However, this kind of interdependence does not come easily to most of us in Britain, and often our culture works against us in this. We are a highly mobile society where many of us commute long distances to work daily and even expect to move cities several times in our working lives. Putting down emotional roots in such a transient setting is not easy for us. The ever-growing privatisation of home ownership and the vast number of single households has only increased this sense of isolation. Relationships are the great time-consumer. It has been suggested that nowadays it often seems to be easier to have our "relationships" with the characters in our favoured television programmes than with real people, who make demands on us!

If church services on Sundays are our only time with the community of God's people, it is not very easy sharing our lives authentically with one another in the five minutes after the morning service —before the children start climbing the walls for Sunday lunch!

Friendship or fellowship?

When was the last time you heard a sermon about friendship? I genuinely cannot remember ever having received teaching exclusively about friendship, and I have heard a LOT of sermons over the years! I recently attended a large Christian festival, where the opportunity for prayer ministry (generally understood as the offer to pray with someone following a meeting) is usually available. I was looking forward to having the chance to be ministered to in an anonymous capacity. However as the "prophetic words" were offered I realised that not a single one was applicable to me, as they were all about receiving prayer for problems in your marriage, or issues with your children, or becoming a Christian. I am not married, I do not have children and

I am already a Christian, but I would still like to have been prayed for! Now the issue is not whether I am married or not, the issue is that in our attempt to affirm marriage in a society where marriage is so severely undermined, perhaps the church has neglected to affirm the precious state of friendship that is extolled throughout the Scriptures.

Biblical friendship is not seen as a "prelude" to marriage but as a life-giving end in itself, both before and after marriage. So many marriages are put under unnecessary pressure because one partner is expecting the other to fulfil all their mental and emotional needs.

The most famous of all the biblical models of friendship is, of course, the story of David and Jonathan.[2] Contemporary readers of the story often struggle with the intimacy that David and Jonathan shared, sometimes believing that they must have had a sexual relationship; however I think such a reading of these passages reveals more about us than it does about them! Why does the idea of intimate friendship outside of marriage surprise us so much? We are created for deep, life-giving relationships with one another. We all have an inner longing to know and be known by others, and such intimacy does not have to have a sexual identity to it.

There seems to be so much confusion in the church about what friendship actually is and is not, and it is probably helpful to make a distinction at this stage between "fellowship" and "friendship". "Fellowship" —most of us are clueless about the meaning of that word! I was baptised at the end of my first year at university, and after the baptismal ceremony I had the "right hand of fellowship" extended to me by the church leader! I am pretty sure that I had no idea what it meant then, but I later discovered how fellowship is described in so many ways in the New Testament: in the Acts of the Apostles, the epistles of Paul and in 1 John, characterising our mutual relationships with our fellow believers in the light of our relationship with the Father because of what Jesus has done. God has accepted us, and we accept each other. As Christians we are called into this fellowship with other Christians throughout the world. It is an awesome privilege to be able to meet Christians we have never met before – even on the other side of the world – knowing that we are in fellowship with one another, as brothers and sisters of the same Father. The same applies locally; we are called by God to encourage and honour one another —but that does not mean that suddenly we all become best friends!

Encouragement

Encouragement literally means "to put courage in". Thinking back to the image of the pilgrimage, we can see how pilgrims might have been able to put courage back into fellow pilgrims, by watching out for hostile forces when the terrain became difficult. When the journey seemed to stretch on without end, pilgrim bands would play music and worship together as they travelled, to remind each other of their final destination and the purpose of their journey.

> And let us consider how we may spur one another on towards love and good deeds. Let us not give up meeting together, as some are in the habit of doing, but let us encourage one another —and all the more as you see the Day approaching.
> *Hebrews 10:24f.*

Here we see that, for Christians, being together – meeting together – and encouraging one another seem to be inextricably linked.

Encouragement can be given and received on different levels. By just physically being together we can receive encouragement, as we discover that we are not alone on our journey. Each summer our church youth group joins 15,000 other young people at the *Soul Survivor* festival. Yes, it means you go for a week with next to no sleep and yes, you will have to queue at some ridiculous hour in the morning if you want a shower! Yet all of these minor inconveniences fade away in comparison with the encouragement our youth group receives in knowing that there are at least 15,000 other teenagers out there who are sharing their "journey" with them.

However, this passage from the letter to the Hebrews is talking less about whether we come to a church service on Sunday or an annual festival, and more about whether we are living our lives with sufficient closeness and openness to others, that we can see the work of God in the lives of our fellow Christians. As we see "up close" how God is giving grace to others in difficult times, or how they are enjoying the faithfulness of God in abundant times, we receive courage once again for our long journey which sometimes passes through some hostile terrain. So, there can be the general encouragement of being together with the people of God as well as a more specific encouragement that is received by sharing our lives on a more intimate level.

Exhortation

Of course there will be a finite number of people with whom we will be able to share our lives on this deeper level, but these relationships will be based on more than encouragement alone. If we return to the letter to the Hebrews we read the challenge, "… let us consider how we may spur one another on towards love and good deeds." When I think of "spurring" I immediately think of horse riding and how the rider digs their spurs into the horse to get it to go faster. This has always struck me as probably a painful thing —but it is a highly effective image, and an especially helpful one when we consider how we might express intimate friendship. Tolerance is given high value in the public discourse of contemporary Britain. Individualism and pluralism often seem to make it unacceptable to state ethical and value judgements which are at the heart of Christianity. As the people of God we are called to more than a life of mere tolerance —we are called to "spur one another on"; to "admonish one another", and even to "rebuke and encourage" —though, of course, only with "great patience and careful instruction". (See Colossians 3:16; 2 Timothy 4:2.) Like the spurring of a horse, this can be a painful business, but it can sometimes prove the only way to help us move beyond spiritual adolescence to becoming fully mature in Christ. (See Ephesians 4:11–16.)

A short while ago I ran a half marathon. It was a life-time achievement and one that I promised myself I would never repeat! In order to train for the event I knew that I would have to find a running partner to keep me on schedule. Although we were total strangers when we started training together, we saw each other through torrential rain, early mornings, dark evenings and a multitude of aches and pains. We made a deal with each other, that whatever happened on race day we would stick together throughout the whole course. Now thirteen miles might not sound a lot to you, but it is a lot to me! I could have quit with "stitch" at four miles, dehydration at seven miles, tedium at ten miles and sheer agony at twelve miles —but we had made this deal to stick together. At every painful landmark my running partner had the opportunity to just agree with me and say, "I know how you feel, it must be awful; let's quit!" I might have thought she was a nice sympathetic person at the time, but I would not have finished the race, achieved my life-time goal and have the tee shirt to prove it!

Yet we do this all the time as fellow believers. When we start to get "stitch" or "dehydration" with the effort of running our race, or when our journey with Christ seems just plain tedious, or when obeying God is costly, and the pain just does not seem worth it, we are often too quick to sympathise and not quick enough with our "spurs".

Running partners

The Book of Proverbs has much to say about friendship, but one of the less palatable verses on the theme is Proverbs 27:6,

> Wounds from a friend can be trusted,
> but an enemy multiplies kisses.

As my friend puts it, "It's important to have people in your life who are more interested in your holiness than your happiness." We all need "running partners" who will not just sympathise with us when being faithful to God is proving painful, costly, or just plain tedious. Intimate friendship and true loyalty must have a dimension that is prepared to challenge or even rebuke, in order that we can both finish our "race" together. This is one of the profound qualities which can mark enduring Christian love. Of course, for this aspect of friendship to work as it should, the motive must be genuinely selfless loving concern for the other's true spiritual wellbeing.

The word "accountability" has had a bad press in the church of recent years. Some still think of accountability as synonymous with the heavy shepherding movement, that seemed to disempower Christians, inhibiting them from making decisions or taking initiative without first referring to others, who were given a great deal of authority. Although the extremism of this movement may sometimes have proved damaging, the principle of "giving an account" for the actions and decisions we make can be a very liberating one.

Every few months I meet with a group of three other girls for a weekend, for the express purpose of sharing our lives, praying for each other and being "accountable" to one another. We all have quite different jobs, different temperaments, and live in different cities, but we have made it a priority to meet together regularly. Our times together do not usually stretch from one spiritual high to the next, but we have had the privilege of being involved deeply in one another's lives and seeing one another mature in Christ. We have an expectation that we will be as open about our lives as we can possibly be, and we have given each other permission to challenge and correct one another where necessary. There is nothing original about what we do when we meet together. Christians have been sharing their lives in this way for centuries. (Early Methodism used the principles of such groups.) However, I have found that such "intentional friendship" is not something that will naturally emerge over time but usually needs to be invited. If the Holy Spirit is to be at the centre of the proceedings we cannot be overly prescriptive about how our time together should be spent, but many such groups do find it helpful to use a set of questions to ask one another when they meet, such as these:

* Is Jesus real to me?
* Did the Bible live for me today?
* Am I moving in the power of the Spirit?
* Am I fulfilling God's calling on my life?
* Do I have healthy relationships with my peers, my leaders and the opposite sex?

* Am I a slave to work, friendships, hobbies or habits?
* Am I eating and sleeping well? Am I taking enough rest?
* Am I walking with integrity?
* Is there anybody whom I fear, criticise, hold resentment towards? If so, what am I doing about it?
* How do I handle stress?
* Do I manage my money well?
* Am I defeated in any area of my life, impure, critical or jealous?[3]

Such questions take us beyond polite "prayer partnerships". They force us to consider how we are displaying "love and good deeds", they search us if we are open to self-deception and help us to see whether we are living lives that are honouring to Jesus. In such relationships we make ourselves vulnerable to one another, as we open ourselves up to the potential abuse of the issues we might share. However, as trust is gradually earned through the sensitive care of each of the others, these friendships can be the means of deep encounter with God and one another.

Endurance

Friendship can be one of the most significant means of experiencing God's grace in our lives, but moving beyond polite superficiality is always costly. Most close friendships experience times of disillusionment as we move beyond superficiality to authenticity. Mistakes are made, sensitive issues are misunderstood or mishandled, and each time we have to choose whether to extend or withhold forgiveness. Unconditional friendship is time-consuming and demanding, and often a private spirituality that does not involve anyone other than God can seem deeply appealing!

We know that our position in Christ is for eternity, and that our discipleship here needs to be marked by patient endurance. We have been given the great gift of the fellowship of other Christians, and we are called to give and receive friendship and encouragement, to help one another to stay true to the path of faithful discipleship. We may not all belong to the sort of organized friendship group I have described, but each one of us needs to know that we are not alone —we really are members of one body, precious and loved by Jesus.

Notes

[1] 1 Corinthians 12:12–31.

[2] See 1 Samuel 20.

[3] The basic premise for many of the questions is of shedding light on areas of sin or deception that may otherwise stay hidden and continue to exert power over us if we were to contend with these issues in isolation. (See 1 John 1:6–7.)

I perhaps should mention that I make no claim to originality with this list! The questions have been used elsewhere, in various forms.

10

RECYCLING GRACE

Tom Peryer

Relationships which do not endure, which are fractured, damaged or broken, are at the heart of most of the world's suffering —in families, communities, nations and between neighbours. In a survey, 21,000 people across the world were asked what things most affected their wellbeing —what was most likely to make them feel happy or unhappy. The highest indicator was relationships with others, which came ahead of physical appearance, physical health, beliefs, sex and material possessions.

Sadly, even the church sometimes suffers from broken relationships and internal divisions, many of which are very widely publicised, affecting the way the world views what we are saying and doing. Recently, I made a presentation to a charity to ask the trustees for some money for a new church school, and at the meeting I was grilled by twelve people. Mostly it was just polite questioning, but one member of the interviewing panel said, "You speak of wanting to establish a school based on Christian values, but it seems to me the Church of England is in deep schism and terminal decline over its values and what it believes. Why should we give any money to that sort of organisation?" Many Christian leaders will have heard similar things, and such questions are asked of many denominations.

On that same day as that meeting took place I attended a celebration of Richard Bewes' ministry of twenty two years at All Souls, Langham Place in London. Asked to mention some high points of his time there, Richard referred not to some of the great occasions but to, "...the marvellous unity that we have enjoyed here over all this time, with no dissension, rifts, walk-outs." His ministry there has been a powerful and enduring relationship with his congregation and his staff team of over forty! We are reminded that there are many parish churches where the gospel is preached, the Bible is believed and people are bearing witness faithfully, in unity. But the church shares with human societies generally the struggles that are involved in maintaining enduring love.

The sustaining of enduring love and relationships requires grace —God's free gift.

"Grace and peace to you from God our Father and the Lord Jesus Christ", writes Paul in Philippians 1:2 and, in the last verse of the final chapter of the epistle, "The grace of the Lord Jesus Christ be with your spirit." What is this grace? Well Paul gives a beautiful definition of it in another letter he wrote, this time to the Christians in Corinth. In 2 Corinthians 8:9 he writes, "For you know the grace of our Lord Jesus Christ, that though he was rich, yet for your sakes he became poor, so that you through his poverty might become rich." And earlier in Philippians Paul quotes a line from one of the very first Christian hymns, saying that "...he made himself nothing...." So the grace of Jesus is seen in his generous offering of himself and all his riches. Grace is generosity, and generosity must surely be one of the qualities which distinguish an enduring relationship. It was certainly something that characterised the mutual relationship between the apostle Paul and the community of all the saints in Philippi. From the day when Paul had first set foot in Europe there in Philippi, and a haberdasher and a jailer had been converted, the church and Paul had a very warm and enduring relationship. And on more than one occasion, those Philippian Christians had sent money and gifts to help other Christians and Paul himself. In fact one of the purposes of this letter had to do with their sending of gifts via Epaphroditus to Paul, when he was in prison in Rome.

Generosity

Generosity and giving are characteristic of God, and of the gospel. Generous giving is one of the first consequences of love. What is the most famous Gospel verse? "For God so loved the world that he gave his one and only Son, that whoever believes in him shall not perish but have eternal life" (John 3:16). Love is meaningless unless it is demonstrated in actions, and perhaps most of all in giving, and God's giving is not just a routine giving, it is generosity beyond our imagining. So as we consider how to find, foster and express enduring love in the context of enduring relationships, we see immediately how giving and going on giving must have a high priority in sustaining such love.

Consider the parable that is most expressive of the gospel of generous grace —the parable of the prodigal son. When the son came to his senses and returned home, he was not only received, allowed back in, he was welcomed with a generosity of spirit and gifts which were far more than he deserved. This is, of course, the point of the gospel. Grace is undeserved. That is not fair! It is not proportionate; it is not measured! The Father gives lovingly to his wayward son. James writes of God (who we can ask for wisdom),

"...who gives generously to all without finding fault." It is this model which we are expected to follow.

Indeed it was there at the very beginning. In Deuteronomy 15:7ff, the Jews as individuals and as a people are told: "If there is a poor man among your brothers in any of the towns of the land that the Lord your God is giving you, do not be hard-hearted or tight-fisted towards your poor brother. Rather be open-handed and freely lend him whatever he needs.... Give generously to him and do so without a grudging heart...."

There are a number of ways in which we can be generous, both to those close to us and to the wider Christian community. The most obvious is the one that we have just observed —the giving or sharing of our material wealth. There should be an element in every Christian's life of planned generosity— looking at your income and possessions and resolving to give a generous portion of that away. As you know, a tenth is often used as a benchmark for Christians. The Church of England, always looking for the middle way, suggests that 5% of net income would be a good target to aim at!

When it comes to giving, frequently the most generous people are those who have least, as the story of the poor widow with her two small coins illustrated. Which is the poorest continent in the world? Africa. But any visitor to Africa who meets ordinary people will tell of their extraordinary generosity to guests.

There was a famous Cornish miner and lay preacher called Billy Bray, famous for saying, "If they tried to shut me up and put me in a barrel I should shout 'Glory' through the bunghole." He had little by way of material possessions, and one day his wife sent him to the manager of the pit to borrow ten shillings. On his way back he stopped off to see a family who were even more needy than his own family, so he lent them five shillings. Then he called on another family and found the same thing there, so he lent that one five shillings and thus returned home empty-handed. His wife was much exasperated, but three days later someone gave the family a pound. "There's the ten shillings and ten shillings interest," said Billy.

That was an example of spontaneous giving. The gift that comes at some unexpected time, rather than on a birthday or at Christmas, probably gives more pleasure than the expected ones because of the element of surprise. Even long-lasting relationships benefit from spontaneous gifts to keep the relationship alive and well (even if sometimes they are peace offerings).

Generosity of action

As well as being generous with material things and our money, there needs to be a generosity of action. Everyone has things we have to do and are expected do, in terms of our family, our work colleagues, our neighbours. For parents it might mean endless getting up in the night; giving lifts; inviting people around for a meal; offering to do someone's ironing for them; taking stuff to the dump for someone who has no car; helping to decorate someone's house for them; sitting listening to someone when you have got 101 things that need doing; spending some extra time with someone after school; running clubs and coaching teams; going on a soup run; giving up some holiday time to work on a Christian activity. Generosity of action means going the extra mile for people even when you really do not feel like doing so, and even when it is not appreciated. In Paul's letter to the Galatians, he exhorts them, "Let us not become weary in doing good, for at the proper time we will reap a harvest if we do not give up. Therefore, as we have opportunity, let us do good to all people, especially those who belong to the family of believers" (Galatians 6:9f).

Generosity of attitude: gratitude

To sustain enduring love, generosity of action needs to be combined with gratitude of heart. In our relationships it is all too easy to focus on what is wrong with the other person. One of the things that happens when relationships are fractured – sometimes ending up in a divorce or people not speaking to each other – is that people have forgotten those things which attracted them to each other in the first place, and begin only to see those things which irritate, anger or frustrate them about the other. So it is important to focus on what is good, attractive and admirable.

Again, we need to look first to the example of Jesus. He gave his life that we might live; he forgave generously; he healed generously; his self-giving in obedience to the Father was total. He taught the disciples to have a generous attitude, too. Oblivious to their own personal safety, they were to set out and preach the good news of the kingdom for the benefit of others. They were taught to forgive generously, without limit, to heal the sick and to minister no matter what the dangers. And of course, throughout the Acts of the Apostles and the epistles we see exactly the same attitude being lived out in practice by Christians. The attitude of all disciples, then and now, is supposed to be like that of Christ Jesus.

We know that we are to focus not on others' negative character traits, but instead look for what is good. This is indeed a generous attitude to adopt, not least with those with whom we have close or familial relationships, whether spouse, sibling, parent or close working colleague. With such people it is all too easy to concentrate on the negative aspects of their character, largely ignoring much that is good. This reminds me of a talk given by a friend to a church group. He held up a sparklingly white, large card with a black dot near the middle. He asked them for comments about his visual aid. Everyone remarked on the black dot near the middle, none about the rest of the dazzlingly white card. Understandable, you might say. Often we can be like that, concentrating on one blemish and ignoring what is good. Frequently, that is how we see those closest to us, ignoring what is good and concentrating only on the weak or irritating points. The quickest way by which we can remain positive about those closest to us is through continually showing gratitude.

A national newspaper recently featured the findings of a book entitled *The Best Kept Secret*, by Dr Janet Reibstein, a clinical psychologist. Her book, written from a secular point of view, is a study of what makes relationships endure, particularly in the context of a divorce rate which is still rising, following a few years of slight decline. In some ways her findings are not earth shattering, though they are based on exhaustive research of enduring married relationships. She concludes that those partners who protect each other, who do things together – such as eating, sleeping and experiencing enjoyment together – and who set apart time with each other, maybe taking one meal just as a couple together each week (even when children are around), are more likely to stay in a committed relationship with one another. She also observed that it is all too easy to leave out gratitude. Omitting simple but vitally important things such as saying thank you for meals which the other has prepared, and for mundane domestic tasks carried out, can soon lead to loss of respect, and a corresponding growth in resentful attitudes. She noticed that if there is an absence of such generosity of spirit, expressed in gratefulness, then the middle years of life may see unfaithfulness. Although her conclusions, based as they are on careful observation, are utterly true, it is instructive to note how they relate to the pattern laid down in the New Testament for good and beneficial relationships. That pattern is best expressed by the kind of loving summarised by Paul in the familiar passage about love in 1 Corinthians 13:4ff., which expresses so much about the quality of enduring love. Although the word gratitude is not explicitly mentioned there, thanksgiving and generosity permeate the whole body of Paul's teaching.

So in our relationships we must preserve gratitude. But that is more easily said than done. Like most aspects of loving, it results from both care and discipline. Like a package of glass sent through the post, we need to constantly remind ourselves that relationships especially need to be "handled with care". There is a delightful old story which reminds us that gratitude, like other aspects of loving, needs to be cherished and practised. A mother takes her little two year old son for a day at the beach. He is wearing the right clothing to protect him from the sun —including a sun hat. A tremendous wave suddenly washes the small boy into the sea, whereupon his mother, greatly distressed, cries out to God, "Lord, I beg you, please bring my son back... Never again will I complain about anything." Just as she finishes her prayer, another huge wave crashes down. As it retreats, she sees that her son has been thrown back onto the beach, rather startled but none the worse for his experience. She looks at the boy, then up at the sky, and calls out, "And where is his hat?" How easily gratitude can be submerged in our incessant demands!

If we have learnt to be grateful to God for his lavish grace, and continue to be grateful to him every day for his acceptance of us in Christ, then this is the bedrock of a generally thankful heart— seeing everything good as coming from his hand: our food, shelter, work, friends and closest relationships. If on the other hand we see these blessings as ours as of right, then the seedbed for gratitude does not exist as it should.

What I hope we have seen in this final chapter is that to sustain enduring relationships is to share in a cycle of grace in which we ourselves first receive acceptance as a result of God's unfathomable grace to us, and then offer generosity to others, through word and action. Aware of his great generosity to us, we may in turn be grateful to him and for those he has given us to be with. Sustaining close enduring relationships is so great a task that nothing less than daily recourse to his love and grace will do. Some who read this book may be facing a crisis or having difficulty in keeping an important relationship peaceful, fruitful and rewarding. If this is the case, then the best advice I can give here is this: discover for yourself that you are loved by God for who you are; and, if you go to him with your pain, problem, or even sense of failure, his response is not to condemn but to help —indeed to embrace you as a person with whom he wants to have the most enduring of all relationships, into eternity.

Remember that moment when the prodigal son returned, feeling that he had broken his filial relationship with his father by greed, independence, ingratitude and the selfish pursuit of pleasure. The father, "...saw him and was filled with compassion for him; he ran to his son, threw his arms around him and kissed him." We ourselves need to receive that overwhelming and undeserved grace; then it can be "recycled" to others, and above all to those with whom we want to have relationships of enduring love.

POSTSCRIPT

We have looked at the need to nourish enduring love in our lives. We have seen that learning to love in this way involves, amongst many other things, no doubt: fulfilling promises; learning to listen; showing affection; expressing caring love in the communities to which we belong; remaining faithful in friendship; exercising forgiveness; showing gratitude and generosity. So we have seen something of the qualities needed in enduring love.

If this study has assisted, even a little, in helping you to appreciate how enduring relationships may be sustained and nourished, then it will have achieved its purpose. Above all, if it helps you to look to him who has shown his love as being supremely a covenant-making love, which has been made known to those in every generation who call upon him – then it will have pointed you to the source of all enduring love.

Only he can enable us to love with a love like his —a love that endures forever.

CHAPTER BY CHAPTER BIBLE STUDY GUIDE

It could be that small study or fellowship groups might like to use the book as a study guide to the theme of enduring love. In that case, the Bible passages below could be used in such studies and, together with the chapter itself, provide material for fellowship or study group discussions.

1. **Love and Faithfulness**
Psalm 85 and Psalm 145
2. **Fulfilling Promises**
Genesis 15:1–16; Psalm 15; Ecclesiastes 5:1–7;
Matthew 5:33 –37; 2 Corinthians 1:12 – 24
3. **Learning to Love**
Psalm 145; John 13:1–17; 1 Corinthians 13:1–13;
Philippians 1:7–11
4. **Learning to Listen**
Psalm 27; 1 Kings 19:9–18; Ecclesiastes 5:1–7;
James 1:19–25
5. **Demonstration of Affection**
Song of Songs 2 – 3:5; Philippians 2:1– 4
6. **Learning to Change**
2 Corinthians 3:17–18; Galatians 5:16 –26; Romans 8:1–17
7. **Belonging to Community**
Romans 12:9 –12; Colossians 3:12–17; 1 Peter 3:8 –12
8. **Dealing with Conflict**
Matthew 5:21–26; Matthew 18:21– 35; John 18:28 –19:16
9. **Friendship**
2 Samuel 2:1–27; Proverbs 17:17; 27:6; John 11:1–16
10. **Recycling Grace**
Luke 15:11–32; 2 Corinthians 8:1–9; Philippians 2:1–11;
John 1:1–14